SHAKESPEAREAN METADRAMA

The publication of this book was assisted by the Atkinson Fund

SHAKESPEAREAN METADRAMA

The Argument of the Play in

TITUS ANDRONICUS · LOVE'S LABOUR'S LOST

ROMEO AND JULIET · A MIDSUMMER NIGHT'S DREAM

AND RICHARD II

James L. Calderwood

UNIVERSITY OF MINNESOTA PRESS, MINNEAPOLIS

To Cleo

Preface

WHILE working on this book I have held a grant from the Humanities Institute of the University of California, for which I am grateful. I am also grateful to Professor William H. Matchett of the *Modern Language Quarterly* and to Professor Caroll Camden of *Studies in English Literature* for permission to reprint here, newly corrected and augmented, a couple of early quartos: "*A Midsummer Night's Dream*: The Illusion of Drama," *MLQ*, 26 (1965) and "*Love's Labour's Lost*: A Wantoning with Words," *SEL*, 5 (1965).

Portions of the manuscript have been read, commented on, and (they keep insisting) marvelously improved by colleagues and friends — Hazard Adams, William H. Matchett, James Mc-Michael, Harold E. Toliver, and especially Murray Krieger, whose interest in and in behalf of the book has been steady, and steadily appreciated.

The texts referred to throughout are those in *The Complete Plays and Poems of William Shakespeare*, ed. William A. Neilson and Charles J. Hill (Cambridge, Mass., 1942).

Contents

I   Introduction · Metadrama, Metapoetry, and
Shakespeare   3

II   *Titus Andronicus* · Word, Act, Authority   23

III   *Love's Labour's Lost* · A Dalliance with Language   52

IV   *Romeo and Juliet* · A Formal Dwelling   85

V   *A Midsummer Night's Dream* · Art's Illusory
Sacrifice   120

VI   *Richard II* · The Fall of Speech   149

   Index   187

SHAKESPEAREAN METADRAMA

I

Introduction

SHAKESPEARE provides models for all occasions, especially for those that inform against us. To the critic trying on introductory styles for a book on Shakespearean metadrama (introductory but after the fact) — at one moment consulting his glossary of critical equivocation, at the next heaving himself into his trumpeting stance — the plight of Falstaff at the Boar's Head Tavern comes all too readily to mind. "What trick," he must ask himself, "what device, what starting-hole, canst thou now find out to hide thee from this open and apparent shame?" Abundantly endowed with Falstaff's instinct, if not his wit, and mindful that the interpretive method in this book may produce a lowering of brows, perhaps even a drawing down of blinds, among what Northrop Frye has feelingly called the oh-come-now school of critics, I suspect that the likeliest device is simply to carry one's guts away as nimbly and with as quick dexterity as possible, roaring for mercy the while. Falstaff's evasive devices include taking a kind of diversionary cover behind drama — "What, shall we be merry? Shall we have a play extempore?" — but his fate — for Hal flushes him out of there too, saying "Content, and the argument shall be thy running away" — persuades me of the futility of trying to divert attention from the following interpretations of individual plays by making ostentatious gestures here about the theory of metadrama. No amount of theory, not even good theory, can rescue bad criticism. On the other hand I hope that a certain sketchiness in the way of formal theory will not invalidate the substantive claims of individual interpretations. If it is otherwise, then must I be horribly chid since my notions of metadrama arose somewhat extempore, materializing rather like Falstaff's eleven men in buckram, in the distress of the moment after I had got myself deep enough in to wonder how and why. What follows in the remainder of this chapter, then, are a few speculations sent up from the depths — essays at defining a notion of metadrama and situating it within a general critical as well as a locally Shakespearean context.

II

"Metadrama" is not an altogether satisfactory term for the concept I have in mind because the prefix may suggest to some readers plays that somehow go "beyond" or at least strain at the limits of drama, as though afflicted with a kind of artistic hubris. That to some degree is the meaning of the term "metaplay" or "metatheatre," which has acquired some currency since the appearance of Lionel Abel's book *Metatheatre: A New View of Dramatic Form* in 1963. As the term is used by Abel and others metatheatre is a dramatic genre that does go beyond drama (at least drama of a traditional sort), becoming a kind of anti-form in which the boundaries between the play as a work of self-contained art and life are dissolved.[1] Since it is good terminological tactics to swallow up

1 Some of the critics who have addressed themselves to this general subject are Ernst Curtius in *European Literature and the Latin Middle Ages*, trans. Willard R. Trask (Princeton, N.J., 1953), pp. 138–144; Robert M. Adams in *Strains of Discord* (Ithaca, N.Y., 1958), pp. 52–62; Oscar Büdel in "Contemporary Theater and Aesthetic Distance," *PMLA*, 76(1961):277–291; Anne Righter in *Shakespeare and the Idea of the Play* (London, 1962); Herbert Weisinger, "Theatrum Mundi: Illusion as Reality," in *The Agony and the Triumph* (East Lansing, Mich., 1964); Thomas B. Stroup in *Microcosmos: The Shape of the Elizabethan Play* (Lexington, Ky., 1965); Jackson I. Cope in "The Rediscovery of Anti-Form in the Renaissance," *Comparative Drama*, 2(1968):155–171; and Leslie Epstein in "Beyond the Baroque: The Role of the Audience in the Modern Theater," *Tri-Quarterly*, 12(1968):213–234.

Much of the criticism of *Hamlet* and of the late romances is in this vein. I might mention, somewhat randomly: Maynard Mack's often reprinted article on "The World of *Hamlet*," *Yale Review*, 41(1952):502–523, and his "En-

neighboring concepts, I would be happy to let my notion of meta-drama subsume that of metatheatre; the latter would then become a species of metadrama devoted to exploring the nature of contex-tual form and the function of aesthetic distancing—issues, inci-dentally, with which my analysis of *A Midsummer Night's Dream* is concerned. Still, I would not want to limit metadrama to plays that make forays across or at least like to flirt around the borders between fiction and reality. The more general argument of this book is that Shakespeare's plays are not only about the various moral, social, political, and other thematic issues with which critics have so long and quite properly been busy but also about Shake-speare's plays. Not just "the idea of the play," as in Anne Righter's fine book of that title, but dramatic art itself—its materials, its me-dia of language and theater, its generic forms and conventions, its relationship to truth and the social order—is a dominant Shake-spearean theme, perhaps his most abiding subject.

Everyone knows that Shakespeare fairly early got onto the mas-ter metaphor of life-as-drama and used it extensively to illuminate the experiences of his characters. The big set-piece speeches like Jacques's "All the world's a stage" and Prospero's "Our revels now are ended" are familiar but less common than the transient appear-ances of such terms as act, play the part, counterfeit, shadow, stage, cast, plot, quality, scene, and pageant, each of which momentarily sets the world in the focus of art. Like others, I have made much of these in my interpretations, not to document the fact that Shake-speare has frequent recourse to the terms of his trade, as indeed most Elizabethan dramatists do, but to suggest that such metaphors give us access to a complex and coherent mode of dramatic mean-ing in which Shakespeare constantly works. At the same time,

gagement and Detachment in Shakespeare's Plays" in *Essays on Shakespeare and Elizabethan Drama*, ed. Richard Hosley (Columbia, Mo., 1962), pp. 275–296; C. G. Thayer, "*Hamlet*: Drama as Discovery and as Metaphor," *Studia Neophilologica*, 28(1956):118–129; Richard Foster, "*Hamlet* and the Word," *University of Toronto Quarterly*, 30(1961):229–245; Charles Forker, "Shake-speare's Theatrical Symbolism and Its Function in *Hamlet*," *Shakespeare Quarterly*, 14(1963):215–229; Reuben Brower, "The Mirror of Analogy: *The Tempest*," in *The Fields of Light* (New York, 1951), pp. 95–122; and Nor-man Rabkin's chapter "The Great Globe Itself" in *Shakespeare and the Com-mon Understanding* (New York, 1967), pp. 192–233.

metaphors are reciprocally illuminative; between the metaphor of the play and the play itself there is a meaningful interplay. If Henry VI is figured as a dramatist staging the play of state, how he does and fails to do this can tell us something about how that royal dramatist Shakespeare — in whose theatrical realm actors are courtiers, and groundlings in the pit are subjects as potentially rebellious as Jack Cade's unworthies — regards his role in ordering his fictional commonwealth. If Coriolanus commits himself to a verbal style in which wheat and chaff are thrown indiscriminately together to satisfy his rigid conception of truth, what happens in consequence may be as suggestive for the politics of art as it is for the art of politics. Attending to such metaphors of drama can tell us a good deal not only about individual plays but about Shakespeare's evolving conceptions of his art.

In mentioning Shakespeare's conceptions of his art I seem to be courting a sort of combined intentional-biographical fallacy; and I suppose heretical phrases like "Shakespeare knows" or "intends" or "has in mind" do pop up in the following chapters with disconcerting frequency. I should be quick to say therefore that I am not measuring the plays against certain mysterious intentions of their author to which in the convenient absence of textual evidence I alone have access. Shakespeare's final intentions *are* the play. But if it is more comforting, I hereby empower the reader to substitute for "Shakespeare knows" or "intends" or "has in mind" something like "On the objective evidence of the play itself, painstakingly probed and peered at, we may reasonably infer that Shakespeare must have known or intended or had in mind" etc. "Shakespeare," in other words, comes pretty close to meaning "Shakespeare's works" or "this play." Still, as a kind of unliterary fiction, it is pleasant to think of Shakespeare as having at least temporarily occupied live skin before being permanently bound in calf; and so at the risk of being indulgently nonobjective I do now and again wonder what he thought he was up to. But these wonderings, it must be urged, derive wholly from the plays themselves and bear only on Shakespeare the dramatist from whom the plays derive. It is all wonderfully and deviously circular!

Let me go at it another way. When analyzing a play we have no right to take anything in it as a direct expression of its author, and except for an occasional historian-biographer poaching in literary territories Shakespeare critics have largely suppressed the impulse, as Vladimir Nabokov puts it, to "cause the great man to circulate among the people, ideas, and objects which he himself described and which one pulls out half-dead from his books with which to stuff one's own." [2] They have refrained from doing this because they know that Shakespeare's primary — indeed *only* — loyalties in writing a play were to the play itself, that whatever his attitudes may have been about politics, religion, war, love, roaring boys, etc., they were subdued like the dyer's hand to what they were worked into: dramatic art. This is by now a critical commonplace with respect not only to Shakespearean drama but to poetry in general. Perhaps because it is, however, we have been slow to acknowledge one of its implications — that our critical caveats about reading the poet's beliefs into or out of his poem are founded on arguments that not only admit but authorize one major exception. For no matter how the poet may suppress, transform, or quite dismiss his convictions about outside issues while writing his poem, he can never withhold his convictions about poetry, since it is to these, now embodied in the poem itself, that everything else has been sacrificed. In a sense each poem contains its own poetics.

"Poetics," burdened as it is with a cargo of Aristotelian connotations, is not an entirely happy word here; and I suspect that the idea of a poetics in the poem will, despite my disclaimers, suggest something much more doctrinally self-contained than I intend, as though within the resisting body of each of Shakespeare's plays were lodged an unassimilable and quite possibly malignant lump of foreign matter which on closer inspection begins to look like an octavo of the *Defence of Poesie*. Like Dull in *Love's Labour's Lost*,

2   This appears in an early Nabokov article in *La Nouvelle Revue Française*, March 1937, "Pouchkine ou le vrai et le vraisemblable," according to Andrew Field in *Nabokov: His Life in Art* (Boston, 1967), p. 13. Nabokov, incidentally, is not talking specifically about Shakespeare but about the general tendency of biographers to keep the borders between the author's life and his fictions ill-policed.

however, Shakespeare's plays have "never fed of the dainties that are bred in a book; [they have] not eat paper, as it were." Or if they have, they give evidence of a wonderfully absorptive digestive system. So I am not suggesting that *Romeo and Juliet* or *Twelfth Night* be regarded as a Shakespearean equivalent to Boileau's *Art poétique*, Pope's *Essay on Criticism*, or MacLeish's "Ars Poetica." But I would like to smuggle a slightly diluted version of that idea into the discussion under the label of "metapoetry."

One kind of metapoetry, if I read René Wellek correctly, is versified criticism of the sort just mentioned — ranging from Horace's *Ars Poetica* to Karl Shapiro's *Essay on Rime* — most of which, despite "some aesthetic qualities," is merely discursive prose statement tricked out in such ornaments as meter, rhyme, and imagery to look like poems.[3] This kind of metapoetry is like Abel's

3 René Wellek, "The Poet as Critic, the Critic as Poet, the Poet-Critic," in *The Poet as Critic* (Evanston, Ill., 1967), p. 98. I say "if I read [him] correctly" because it is not entirely clear whether he regards "versified criticism" as one, rather inferior, genre and "metapoetry" as something else, as poems "concerned with the self-definition of the poet and with his mission or function" (p. 98). But apart from the assignment of terms it is merely a question of poems explicitly (versified criticism) or implicitly about poetry; I would call both kinds metapoetry, since, as I go on to point out, even the explicit species has an implicit dimension of metapoetic meaning. (There is, incidentally, a recent anthology called *Poems on Poetry: The Mirror's Garland*, ed. Robert Wallace and James G. Taaffe, New York, 1965.) Murray Krieger's book *A Window to Criticism: Shakespeare's Sonnets and Modern Poetics* (Princeton, N.J., 1964) is a metapoetic treatment of the sonnets, though Krieger does not use the term itself; much of Sigurd Burckhardt's *Shakespearean Meanings* (Princeton, N.J., 1968) is metadramatic criticism of the sort I am describing, though Burckhardt's term is "intrinsic interpretation"; and M. M. Mahood's book *Shakespeare's Wordplay* (London, 1957) is always on the edge of metadramatic criticism, though her preoccupation is with language alone.

In his chapter on "Shakespeare's Games with His Audience" in *The Rape of Cinderella* (Bloomington, Ind. and London, 1970), pp. 100–119 — a book I ran across after this one was in press — Eugene Paul Nasser has some fine remarks on Shakespeare's dramatic "tone" or form that would lead nicely into the notion of metadrama. He speaks, for instance, of Shakespeare's "core drama" — the basic dramatic illusion, which is normally realistic but at least faithful to its premises, whether realistic or fantastic — and of another dimension of the play detached from this which observes and comments on it. This second — I would say "metadramatic" — dimension is conditioned by Shakespeare's desire to control his audience's attitudes toward the play, to meditate on the play, to play games with the play, to "explore more fully the wider

metatheatre, the prefix being taken in the strictest sense: plays that go beyond drama to merge with life, poems that become nonpoetic in addressing themselves to criticism. But metapoetry need not refer merely to poems that in trying to swallow the carp of poetics find themselves sharked into the maw of literary criticism. The prefix may suggest poems that go beyond themselves not by becoming something other than poetry but by acquiring a kind of detachment that enables self-reflection. Detachment ought not of course imply a disjunction or Platonic dualism in the poem; the poetics in the poem is as intrinsic and deeply inwrought as any other kind of meaning. This is true even of metapoems explicitly devoted to poetics. MacLeish's direct statements in "Ars Poetica" about silence, motionlessness, and non-meaning in poetry in no way exhaust the poetics in his poem. After all, the star witness for the view of modern critical theory that form and content are interpenetrative would surely be the poem whose content is itself poetics. In such a poem (though only more obviously than in others) style and form inevitably create instead of contain meaning. For instance, although "Ars Poetica" explicitly states that poems "should not mean/ But be" it nowhere says (apart from urging wordlessness in the first section and motionlessness in the second) how they should be. On the evidence of statement alone we might well assume that MacLeish is advocating poems that "are" as nature "is" — a species of anti-poem, perhaps, that strives by ignoring traditional concepts of literary form to free itself from the dominion of art and return somehow to unmediated existence, raw life, etc. Nevertheless, how poems should be is implicit in the very how — the form and style — of "Ars Poetica" itself, which in its highly symmetrical structure, stringent economy of phrase, and concentration on the visual and tactile image indicates that MacLeish wants poems that aspire not to the condition of mute and formless "being" but to the conditions of the plastic arts, notably painting and sculpture.

implications of any theme or situation that is impelling his core action, and to take the audience along with him in his meditations" (p. 101).

So perhaps one could argue that all poems are implicitly and a few explicitly metapoems. Perhaps the self-regarding aspect of the metapoem is a quality of beauty itself, from lovely ladies to lyrics, which in cherishing its own form and feature would imperialize its autism, making its little room an everywhere. The special world of mood and import fashioned in the poem preempts all others and demands of us as our price of entrance that we deliver ourselves up wholly and as though forever to its spell. And I suppose the principles by which it fashions its world make their implicit claims too in the domain of poetics, appropriating all other poems to itself — an aesthetic categorical imperative (*après moi, moi!*) — much as most poets when acting as critics tend to elevate their own idiosyncrasies to the status of universal law.

But Shakespeare is doing more than merely inadvertently disclosing what all poets must disclose in the process of writing a poem. No play written in words can avoid telling us something about its author's dispositions toward language, but *Love's Labour's Lost*, notoriously preoccupied with the uses and abuses of the poet's medium, is written not only in but about words. Again, no play can avoid revealing certain assumptions and expectations concerning its audience, but *A Midsummer Night's Dream* explores the nature of dramatic illusion as the point of convergence for play and audience and does so with an almost Pirandello-like engrossment in the epistemology of the theater. Nor are these isolated, perhaps half-accidental instances. The Ben Jonson who wrote

> Yet must I not give Nature all: Thy Art,
> My gentle Shakespeare, must enjoy a part

knew very well (unlike Stephen Dedalus) that no one ever hacked blindly at a block of wood and produced a cow that would make Praxiteles envious. Shakespeare's concern, even obsession, with art in his plays casts him less as a natural genius who by virtue of an unconscious metaphoric endowment managed to do all things for all times than as a highly sentient and often downright cunning writer who knew precisely what he was doing.

What he was doing, as Jonson's distinction between the natural and the artful in literary works implies,[4] was two things simultaneously — making-an-*illusion* and *making*-an-illusion. All dramatists do the same, but it seems natural that Shakespeare, capable as we all know of adopting multiple perspectives toward anything, could hardly help thinking of, say, a character both as a realistic person in a realistic world and as a device fashioned by himself to insert into an artificial environment in such a way as to satisfy the necessities of a literary and theatrical structure.[5] This would seem especially true for a playwright working as he did in constant contact with a theatrical company. The fact that the fine forms of the creative imagination can be concretely realized only on the public stage with all its debasing resistances (and, he came increasingly to know, with all its rich resources) would have been in daily evidence to him as he helped route his own or another man's script ("Have you the lion's part written?") through actors who were his friends ("tell them that I Pyramus am not Pyramus, but Bottom the weaver"), into a theater ("This green plot shall be our stage, this hawthorn-brake our tiring house"), and before an audience ("Will not the ladies be afeard of the lion?"). Given his unique standpoint as actor, playwright, and later housekeeper of the theater — a standpoint so radically different from that of the nondramatic poet in relation to *his* art — a play would have for him, I should think, something of the in-and-outness of psychologists' ambiguous figures, at one moment receding from him into its own seemingly autonomous fictive reality and at the next extrorsing to present itself

4   The distinction is brought out more obviously in the succeeding two lines, "For though the Poet's matter, Nature be,/ His Art doth give the fashion," which are of course from Jonson's eulogy to Shakespeare printed as part of the front matter to the First Folio.

5   In his chapter on "The Great Globe Itself" in *Shakespeare and the Common Understanding* Norman Rabkin finds Shakespeare heightening the ambiguity of art-nature in drama — especially in *Pericles* and *Cymbeline* — or driving a wedge between the two in order to "make us recognise the game he is playing" (p. 210), and the game is metadrama, which he plays with much greater skill in *A Midsummer Night's Dream*, *The Winter's Tale*, and *The Tempest*.

as his dependent, a tenuous extension of his own playwriting and directorial skills.[6]

Not just characters of course but all that enters a play — language, actions, historical events, actors, stage properties, etc. — has this curious ambiguity about it (what might be called, to distinguish it from ordinary ambiguities, "duplexity"). Consider for instance, as Shakespeare evidently did, the implications of so lowly a theatrical resource as the three-legged joint stool. In *A Midsummer Night's Dream* (2.1.52–53), *1 Henry IV* (2.4.418), *King Lear* (3.6.55), and *Macbeth* (3.4.68) the joint stool is employed as the most humble, plain, utterly real of objects, the least likely thing to be transformed by somebody's imagination into Puck, a king's throne, Lear's daughter, or Banquo's ghost. "Why do you make such faces?" Lady Macbeth demands; "When all's done,/ You look but on a stool." To be sure, and yet all the audience in the Globe has been looking on is but a stool too. This sudden casting of doubt on the nature and identity of the most innocent of stage props may cause us to wonder naively to whom the stool belongs. Is it the property, quite literally the stage property, of Shakespeare's acting company, the King's Men, or is it fully absorbed into the dramatic

---

6 Eugène Ionesco has some relevant remarks about this in-and-outness of plays, especially when he speaks of how drama at first repelled him because the physical presence of actors and stage, all the *mise en scène* or Aristotelian "spectacle," prevented it from being successful as either realistic illusion or theatrical artifice: "It was as though there were two planes of reality, the concrete, physical, impoverished, empty and limited reality of these ordinary human beings living, moving and speaking on the stage, and the reality of imagination, face to face, overlapping, irreconcilable: two antagonistic worlds failing to come together and unite" (*Notes and Counter Notes*, trans. Donald Watson, New York, 1964, p. 19).

Jackson I. Cope has a good discussion of these antagonistic worlds of drama as seen by various critics, especially Ortega y Gasset (see Cope, "The Rediscovery of Anti-Form in Renaissance," pp. 160–163), and of how the Rennaissance play, capitalizing on this doubleness, becomes what Lionel Abel calls metatheatre: "a little world which refuses to be static, to accept the limitations of minetic form; a little world which mocks aesthetic objectivity as it incorporates the *theatrum mundi* into itself upon its own terms" (p. 168). Brecht's "alienation principle" of course also relies on this dramatic in-and-outness; and Maynard Mack's article on "Engagement and Detachment in Shakespeare's Plays" illustrates how Shakespeare, by manipulating the in-and-outness of the play, controls the psychic distance of the audience.

fiction where it becomes part of the furnishings of Macbeth's castle, an item on his steward's inventory? For the play to succeed as realistic illusion the audience must regard the stool as Macbeth's, which means fictionalizing in their imaginations an object that remains incorrigibly what it was before the play began. The process is analogous to the absorption of language into a literary work. For the language the poet uses comes as drab and gross from the everyday world as Macbeth's joint stool; but it has been transformed by the poetic imagination into a self-enclosed complex of meaning that abandons its referential dependence on the world outside.[7] The joint stool in *Macbeth* undergoes one further transformation — from an object in the Globe theater to an object in Macbeth's castle to the hallucinated ghost of Banquo. Now Macbeth owns it uniquely; it has been wholly interiorized by the fictive world and no longer bears any likeness to its original form; there is no way back from Banquo's ghost to the joint stool owned by the King's Men.[8] Nor is there any route by which we can return from the language of *Macbeth*, whose meanings are uniquely contained in their own ghostly linguistic forms, to the language of Jacobean England from which it came. This is true partly because just as the joint stool becomes Macbeth's by virtue of its insertion into a fictional context — its environment changing but not itself — so language is reconstituted by Shakespeare in *Macbeth* not through any material alteration in words but by virtue of their contextual relations.

Like Theseus in *A Midsummer Night's Dream* ("I never may

7 My translating a visual issue into verbal terms, leaping from ghost to language, may seem somewhat arbitrary, but it mirrors a visual to verbal movement in Macbeth's mind. His lines just following those of Lady Macbeth quoted above are directed first to her and specifically to her visual sense ("Prithee, see there! behold! look!") and then to the ghost itself, whose significance, undiscernible to the startled eye, Macbeth hopes will be manifest in speech ("lo! how say you? . . . If thou canst nod, speak too"). How indeed — not "what" — will the ghost say? Being a product of Macbeth's deed, will it speak his language too? But the ghost keeps its counsel.

8 Another example, to which Harold E. Toliver and I have called attention in *Forms of Poetry* (Englewood Cliffs, N.J., 1968, pp. 5–6), is the transformation of bones and eyes into coral and pearl in Ariel's song (*The Tempest*, 1.2.396ff). Shakespeare can transmute base bone and tissue into coral and pearl in his oceanic-artistic retort, but there is no known alchemical technique by which we may reverse the process.

believe/ These antique fables, nor these fairy toys") or Gertrude in *Hamlet* ("This bodiless creation ecstasy/ Is very cunning in") Shakespeare's audience may respond to art's visionary shapes with a philistine rationalism that refuses to trade the familiar solidity of a joint stool for the dubious insubstantiality of Banquo's ghost. That is, the artist must always deal with those for whom art is merely mimetic, never creative, mirroring back to them in a one-to-one correspondence — joint stool for joint stool — the secure and serviceable world they brought with them to the theater, a world that constitutes the end of their imaginings but only the bare beginning of the poet's. To them — Theseuses, Gertrudes, Lady Macbeths — Shakespeare may well cry with something of Hamlet's anguish, "Do you see nothing there?" and be answered with much of Gertrude's complacency, "Nothing at all, yet all that is I see." Hamlet proves at least temporarily successful in obliging Gertrude to see, if not the ghost of his visiting father, a few moral truths to which she had been oblivious, and Lady Macbeth comes to perceive spiritual realities more persuasive to the guilty eye than the unsullied whiteness of her hand. Perhaps Shakespeare had hopes, then, that his audiences might graduate from a mimetic "all that is I see" to register something of the vast symbolic potency of his plays. If so, it would be because everything in those plays, even the joint stool, has been enlisted in the service of that cause.

Before I provoke an article entitled "How Many Joint Stools Had Lady Macbeth" let me get on to another instance of duplexity: the narrative based on that oldest of organizing devices, the journey. In this sort of work the act of writing "begins" when the hero does, "advances" with his travels, and "ends" when he reaches his goal. A naive author or one who, like Swift in *Gulliver's Travels*, has his sights set on other matters may never remark the duplexity of the journey. Another may give explicit expression to the metaphor once or twice, as Spenser does in the opening and closing stanzas of Canto 12, Book I, *The Faerie Queene* — for example:

> Behold I see the haven nigh at hand,
> To which I meane my wearie course to bend;
> Vere the maine shete, and beare up with the land,

The which afore is fairly to be kend,
And seemeth safe from stormes, that may offend;
There this faire virgin wearie of her way [i.e., Una]
Must landed be, now at her journeyes end:
There eke my feeble barke a while may stay,
Till merry wind and weather call her thence away.

(Stanza 1)

But Spenser fails to exploit the metaphor's potential as a continuous interface between poem as artifice and poem as realistic journey (or in this case "fantastic" journey). On the other hand, if the author is obsessed by the duplexity of art, as I think Shakespeare was, he may conduct his fictive journey so that it reflects the concerns of the adventuring poet as well as the plight of the wandering hero. This is what Robert Penn Warren says Coleridge is doing in the "secondary theme" of *The Rime of the Ancient Mariner*, a theme "in particular about poetry itself" and in general about the creative imagination.[9] And in the chapter on *Romeo and Juliet* I try to show that by having frequent recourse to the voyage metaphor Shakespeare plays with the duplexity of literary form – as both temporal sequence and spatial design – and with the contrary tendencies of the verbal (or retarding) and the actional (or progressive) elements of dramatic art.

External form and internal fiction may so thoroughly interpenetrate in the voyage story that distinguishing one from the other is like distinguishing convexity from concavity in a curved line. Duplexity, however, is by no means limited to journeys. Within the play, figures taken from the lexicon of drama may comment reflexively on the play itself.[10] Shakespeare repeatedly em-

---

9 Robert Penn Warren, "A Poem of Pure Imagination," in *The Rime of the Ancient Mariner* (New York, 1946), p. 104. Meyer Abrams has called attention to a much-used metapoetic notion in his fine article "The Correspondent Breeze: A Romantic Metaphor," *Kenyon Review*, 19(1957):113–130, where he suggests that the breeze "is not only a property of the landscape [in many romantic poems], but also a vehicle for radical changes in the poet's mind."

10 Far and away the most self-reflexive feature of drama is language, which is endlessly susceptible to narcissism by virtue of the number and variety of words that can refer to speech. That does not mean of course that whenever

ploys interior dramatists like Aaron, Oberon, Iago, Prospero, all the kings, whose successes and failures in governing men and events reflect Shakespeare's in governing them. The manipulation of illusions by an Edgar–Poor Tom at Dover cliffs or the staging of a scene of piety by a Richard Crookback may be as metadramatically suggestive as a full-fledged play within a play such as that in *Hamlet* or *A Midsummer Night's Dream*. How a man who kills the king ponders and selects a style in which to kill the king—a Brutus, Hamlet, or Macbeth—may indicate obliquely how Shakespeare, whose imagination is stained with the blood of many kings, has in this play gone about the larger task of marshaling the weapons of tragic art in the cause of death.

Or take a simple knighting, that of the Bastard Faulconbridge in the opening scene of *King John*, which would not seem an especially likely place for metadrama. The usurping John, as we already know, possesses the land (England) rightfully belonging to his nephew, the young Arthur: "Your strong possession," Eleanor says in an aside to John, "much more than your right." The spuriousness of John's title to kingship is further underscored by a quasi-burlesque analogy when the great affairs of state are intruded upon by the Faulconbridges with their dispute over property. The Bastard, because he is a bastard, unjustly possesses the lands belonging to his legitimate half-brother Robert. At this point Shakespeare seems all set to develop a parodying subplot in the popular Elizabethan manner, with the unhistorical Bastard supplying a critique-from-below of the English nobility after the fashion of Jack Cade and his men in *2 Henry VI*, Launce and his dog in *The Two Gentlemen of Verona*, and the servants in *Romeo and Juliet*. But Shakespeare chooses instead to have the Bastard relinquish his title to the land, accept knighthood from John, and go with the King as "Sir Richard" and a Plantagenet. Thus when the newly dubbed Bastard rises Sir Richard, Shakespeare's play rises too. The elevation in social standing is also an elevation in dramatic form as the Bastard

a character uses the word "word" Shakespeare is crystallizing for us his conceptions of language in general or his verbal concerns within the play in particular.

moves from potential subplot figure to main-plot participant and the play moves from a hierarchical, two-level structure to one conducted on a single plane. As a result both the Bastard and Shakespeare are obliged to forgo the easy pleasures of long-distance sniping in favor of the more formidable task (for the Bastard) of coming to terms with a political world in which the final kingly authority is smooth-faced Commodity and (for Shakespeare) of incorporating two dramatic levels of action, each with its distinctive style and ethos, into one complex unity.

The key question for the critic of course is whether what he takes to be self-reflexive metaphors of this sort are indeed such or are merely products of his own tendency to play fast and loose with the literary text. The rich voluptuousness of Shakespearean meaning — which is rather like the multiflected female in Roethke's "Light Listened" who had "more sides than a seal" — will seduce any critic into taking interpretive liberties now and then, and no doubt I have committed my fair share of indiscretions. These will seem to some readers scandalous indeed in the chapter on *Titus Andronicus* where my sustained attention to the metadramatic theme has the look of critical allegorizing. I confess that Shakespeare does seem to me to conduct a prolonged flirtation with something that looks very much like allegory in that play. But if this is allegory — and I'm not at all sure that is the right name for a series of closely related metaphors in which the play mirrors and comments on itself — it seems to be exempt from the complaints often directed at conventional allegory. The latter is usually frowned on because it ultimately shifts our attention away from the play itself; the literal words and actions and characters evaporate as the soul of meaning spirals upward into Platonic heavens, fetching us after. As this flighty figure suggests, allegory of this sort divests itself during its ascent of most sublunary impurities and complexities, winnowing toward an ultimate singleness of meaning which the tunnel-visioned reader is to hunt down, or up, and discover with a sense of consummate finality. Moreover in conventional allegory, as Goethe pointed out in distinguishing it from symbolism, essence precedes existence. There is always an after-thefactness about the allegorical play because its words, actions, characters, etc., derive from a conceptual structure worked out by the playwright-thinker in advance — a structure that the play therefore does not create but merely illustrate.

But the metadramatic theme in, say, *Titus Andronicus* is neither single, separate, nor preexistent. It can in no way precede or exist apart from the play because its subject *is* the play; that is where our attention is compelled to return. If this is allegory it is allegory that is an outgrowth of the creative process itself and fused with the dramatic form to which it both refers and defers. Because of this, because its meanings are thoroughly grounded in the literary substance, the "argument of the play" can make no special claim to thematic priority, nor should it. Far from representing itself as "the" final and somewhat ulterior meaning of the play, as it might if it were allegorically inclined, the metadramatic argument, though sufficiently distinctive to take on a coherence and visibility of its own, is nevertheless merely another of those infinite seallike sides of the Shakespearean dramatic form.[11]

11 How implicit Shakespearean meanings are and how explicitly criticism can render them is perhaps questionable. In this regard I differ somewhat from a critic whose work I very much admire, the late Sigurd Burckhardt, who in the preface to *Shakespearean Meanings* says: "This book is concerned with what Shakespeare *meant*. I believe that Shakespeare's plays, to put it bluntly, have messages and that these messages are discoverable, in fact statable." If these remarks fail to do justice to the often brilliant and always imaginative criticism they preface, still one can sympathize with the impulse "to put it bluntly" and maybe even in terms of statable "messages." Sometimes we seem in danger of claiming that Shakespearean drama is such a deep and dangerous labyrinth of thematic passageways, each concealing minotaurine fallacies awaiting the unstrung critic, that its entrances should be posted "Abandon Hope All Ye Who Enter Here." Abandon hope, that is, of emerging again with anything like a declarative sentence on your lips, let alone a statable message. From literary subtleties so fine and complexities so great as to elude speech we all may at times recoil, as I suppose Burckhardt did. But Burckhardt himself repeatedly demonstrates that Shakespearean meanings are as inextricably embedded in the corporeal substance of dramatic language as the blood in Shylock's hoped-for pound of Antonio's flesh, that such meanings are not directly statable but only at best translatable into the discursive approximations of literary criticism.

We need not view the Shakespearean play either as streetwalker, issuing propositions to all comers, or at the other extreme as fastidious old maid enjoying the elaborately ceremonial but foredoomed courtship of those wizened few of us who have world enough and time. In criticism, as in Shakespeare,

III

If the metadramatic theme is not single in the sense of transcending all other thematic issues, neither is it single within itself. That is, one play may focus on literary style and form, as I think *Romeo and Juliet* does; another play may focus on language and the durability of art, as *Love's Labour's Lost* does; another may focus on poetic versus dramatic language and the immanent truth and power of symbolism, as *Richard II* does; and still another may largely ignore linguistic issues and concentrate instead on the theatrical interaction of playwright, play, and audience, as *A Midsummer Night's Dream* does. In short, each play generates its distinctive metadramatic tensions, and I have tried to let this fact govern my interpretations.[12] If the virtue of this method is that it keeps the idea of metadrama large and flexible enough to respond to Shakespeare's diverse artistic interests as he moves from play to play, one must pay for that virtue, I'm afraid, with at least a partial loss of another — a systematic and unified critical development. Had Shakespeare been gracious enough to write with the needs of his critics in mind, I might have been able to organize a chapter-to-chapter argument that would march with lockstep inevitability toward (surely) apocalyptic conclusions. But it seems obvious in this case that he selfishly refused to develop on all fronts simultaneously, that as in recuperating from an illness there could be only minor advances and retreats here and there along the line and even a complete relapse, a *Merry Wives of Windsor*, once in a while. He must often have found that what the mind knew full well the hand was

there is surely room for a marriage of true minds negotiated through speech, for a bond between poetic and critical languages that productively unites without violating the integrity of either party. If Burckhardt himself has not always done so, still he has — take him for all in all — got those two parties amicably before the altar and fashioned that verbal bond more often than we have any right to expect.

12   A related consideration is the fact that I have no great faith in the chronology of the plays treated. The sequence I have used does no violence to the suppositions generally accepted by my textual, historical, and editorial betters; but chronology makes little real difference anyhow since, as I say, I am less interested in demonstrating historical development — many other plays in this period would have to be considered for that — than in illustrating the interpretive usefulness for particular plays of metadramatic criticism.

too clumsy to realize, and sometimes that the hand held a cunning which, like a perfect golf swing, would not abide the mind's analysis.

For such reasons the chapters to follow are written so that they may be read out of context as individual interpretations, and for such reasons there is no concluding chapter full of epiphanies — only ten lines of Swiftian dots and a marginal explanation from the publisher: "Here the whole scheme of Shakespearean metadrama was compendiously detailed, with an air of great learning and vast shiftiness, but it was not thought fit to print it." In the absence of such a chapter, what I am most anxious to demonstrate, I suppose, is simply a way of looking at Shakespearean drama that perhaps brings into relief a territory of meaning which Shakespeare could hardly have ignored and which we as critics might well explore.

Having labored heroically to disunify the following chapters, let me now try to push them back together a bit by suggesting that, with the qualifications already recorded, there is a kind of argument running through the five plays and hence perhaps an incremental persuasiveness that is best registered if the interpretations are read in sequence. The most recurrent and dominant metadramatic issue in these early plays is one that would trouble any young dramatist who is also a poet: the interplay of language and action in drama. In *Titus Andronicus* a Shakespeare with strong lyric leanings — writer of sugared sonnets and mellifluent narrative poems — who is obliged to stage actions in a theater incorporates into his play metaphors that suggest how poetic language is barbarized by both popular sensationalism and classical authority. The predominance of violent action over language in *Titus Andronicus* is inverted in *Love's Labour's Lost* as Shakespeare attempts to give to the breath of speech a substantiality that will enable it to substitute for action. Wordplay, however, is not sufficient for a stage play, and language must not only be but mean. The failure of dramatic form, of language to unite with action, is marked by the interruptive entrance of the messenger Mercade, who leaves the play in a state of instructive openness. In *Romeo and Juliet* Shakespeare's search for an authentic dramatic style, a true language, leads on the one hand to the self-enclosed verbal world of the lovers and on the other hand to the violent and "airy word" of public speech, from whose noise the lovers seek a sanctuary of silence, ultimately a sanctuary of death. A language is found that can unite the lovers in private marriage but not one that can bind them to their society. Yet in this play Shakespeare seems to move beyond the idea of purely verbal cohesion that had dominated *Love's Labour's Lost* and to sense the binding power of total dramatic form. As the multiple public marriages of *A Midsummer Night's Dream* would imply, incorporating lovers into the larger social fabric is no problem in Theseus's Athens. In this play Shakespeare celebrates his awareness, very likely his discovery, that his art is not fated by the transitory conditions of the theater to fade as soon as it flowers, since to the marriages within the play is added a world-without-end bargain between the play and its audience.

On this happy note of pervasive marriage one might well conclude a book; and Shakespeare, had he been a lesser artist, might well have concluded his dramatic development. But the way forward was not through the repetition of one success. The marriages of *A Midsummer Night's Dream*, which in some degree reflect Shakespeare's sense of having for the first time married all the elements of his art, are followed by the divorces of *Richard II*, which separate not only a king from his queen, his crown, and his life but the poet-dramatist from the world order to which he had been bound by his verbal medium. From here on his conception of order in speech and drama must be framed anew in the writing of each play.

Suiting the action to the word, the word to the action; transcending the temporal limitations of the theater; finding a dramatic style that mediates between the corruptions of public speech and the lyricism of pure poetry; discovering the truth and value of drama — these are abiding issues to which Shakespeare is still addressing himself fifteen years later, though always in different ways. To get a sense of how he develops the argument of the play over that span of time would require a detailed look at a great many works, and that, to paraphrase Berowne, is too long for a book —

this book at least. Like Berowne's play, *Shakespearean Metadrama* exhibits an open form that recognizes the arbitrariness of all endings, certainly the incompleteness of its own argument. Unless I grow virtuous and relent, however, I hope to pursue the argument further at a later date. Meanwhile one rests discontentedly resigned to the wisdom of the old hermit of Prague as reported by Feste: "That that is is."

II

Titus Andronicus

WORD, ACT, AUTHORITY

ALTHOUGH various characters in *Titus Andronicus* have their hands, heads, and tongues lopped off and their bodies pulverized into pasties, it is generally agreed that the most acute suffering occurs among the audience. Thus we can all endorse the request of Aemilius, who materializes out of the carnage near the end of the play and says "You sad Andronici, have done with woes." But having done with woes either in or outside the play seems difficult. At the end Aaron remains buried breast-deep in the ground where he can watch the political order build anew as he starves, and Tamora's body unlike those in the myth of Philomela, Tereus, and Procne undergoes its final anti-Ovidian metamorphosis not into but as a result of birds:

> Her life was beastly and devoid of pity,
> And, being dead, let birds on her take pity.

Critical pity toward Shakespeare has taken a similarly barbaric form in attempts to lop off whichever hand he may have had in the play's composition. T. S. Eliot calls *Titus* "one of the stupidest and most uninspired plays ever written, a play in which it is incredible that Shakespeare had any hand at all." [1] Maybe less than a hand but enough at least to have given "some Master-touches to one or two

[1] T. S. Eliot, "Seneca in Elizabethan Translation," *Selected Essays 1917–1932* (New York, 1932), p. 67.

of the Principal Parts or Characters" in a play by a "private Author," as Edward Ravenscroft claimed when in 1686 he gave some master touches of his own to an adaptation of *Titus*. Or perhaps Shakespeare collaborated with Peele or Kyd or someone else whose literary depravities overcame his own native gentleness. But alas, all attempts at authorial disintegration must encounter Meres's listing of the play as Shakespeare's in *Palladis Tamia* and the even more resistant fact of its inclusion in the First Folio.

However, if we are obliged to admit that Shakespeare *did* write *Titus*, we can still ask how *could* he write it — a brew of horrors seemingly concocted on the witches' recipe in *Macbeth*: "Round about the cauldron go;/ In the poisoned entrails throw." One way of accounting for the sensationalism of the play is to thrust its date of composition as far back as possible toward a bin of self-exonerating juvenilia by assuming, for instance, that Ben Jonson's loose temporal references to it in his Introduction to *Bartholomew Fair* (1614) — "five-and-twenty or thirty years [ago]" — clearly establish a date between 1584 and 1589. This despite the fact that in subject and style the play has obvious affinities to *Lucrece* and *Venus and Adonis*, that Henslowe's diary records as "ne" a production of it by Sussex's men in January 1594, and that later in 1594 the first quarto (*The Most Lamentable Romaine Tragedie of Titus Andronicus*) came ponderously forth. An easier way of accounting for it, however, is simply to deny its badness, though not everybody can speak with Tillyard of the "measured precision" of the play's events, its "masterly" plotting, or its "beautiful lyrical passages," and very few indeed would want to argue that its "very violences are exquisitely proportioned." [2] Far more representative is J. C. Maxwell's remark: "It is, I think, the one play of Shakespeare which could have left an intelligent contemporary in some doubt whether the author's truest bent was for the stage." [3]

2 E. M. W. Tillyard, *Shakespeare's History Plays* (London, 1944), p. 138. Since Tillyard twice refers to the eating of only one son of Tamora at the Thyestean banquet, he appears not to have lingered too attentively over the violence, despite its exquisiteness.

3 "Introduction" to *Titus Andronicus*, ed. J. C. Maxwell (London, 1953), p. xlv.

This seems to me the place to begin, since I wonder if we should assume that such a doubt was available to an intelligent contemporary but not to Shakespeare himself. Why after all should he, lacking our temporal advantage, automatically assume that he was cut out to be a dramatist? Later on, in apparent reference to the theatrical life to which he had so fully devoted himself, he can chide Fortune that

> did not better for my life provide
> Than public means which public manners breeds.
>
> (Sonnet 111)

And at this time, very early on, he may well have been unsure whether Fortune intended him to write for the theater or in literary modes less likely to subdue his nature and manners to what they worked in. "This time," though it is not crucial to my argument,[4] I take to be around 1593, somewhere in the period from June 1592 to May 1594 when the London theaters were almost continuously shut down because of plague and when Shakespeare most likely wrote *Venus and Adonis*, *The Rape of Lucrece*, and an unknown number of sugared sonnets. Returning to drama and addressing himself for the first time to tragedy necessarily meant surrendering certain prerogatives inherent in lyric and narrative poetry. One of these was simply the prestige of poetry, the air of gentility worn by works whose mode of literary existence was private readings among coteries, as contrasted to drama, which outside university circles suffered the disrepute of the common players and of which only a rare exception like *Troilus and Cressida* could get to press without being "sullied with the smoaky breath of the multitude." It is from this refined elevation that Shakespeare calls *Venus and Adonis* "the first heir of my invention" (despite his having written several plays by this time) and attaches an epigraph to the poem that says "Vilia miretur vulgus: mihi flavus Apollo/ Pocula

---

4 It will become apparent, I think, that my reading of the play is not dependent on its date of composition. In some respects my argument would be enhanced if this were Shakespeare's first play. But all that is really necessary is that the writer be a man who was both a poet and a dramatist and not yet in the best sense a poetic dramatist.

Castalia plena ministret aqua" (Let the vulgar admire vile things; for me may golden-haired Apollo provide cups full of water from the Castalian spring). So much for the *Henry VI* plays and probably *The Comedy of Errors*! Clearly, art and the theater lie at opposite poles for him at this stage of his career.

Nevertheless he chooses to write "vile things" in between trips to the Castalian spring, and so must take account of those "vulgar" whose admiration is unfortunately indispensable. The autonomy of speech granted him as poet dissolves the moment he turns playwright. The private poet or even novelist may indulge in self-address, may even shut himself away from his audience like Joyce's Shem and write "over every square inch of the only foolscap available, his own body." But the playwright must shape his words to the lips of the actors and the ears of the audience and, though personally absent from the stage, engage in a dialogue in which his speech is answered immediately with bravos, clapping, hisses, and silence. Thus in a not entirely metaphoric sense he is obliged, unlike Shem, to bring his literary hide before his public, as in the epilogue to *2 Henry IV*: "Here I promised you I would be, and here I commit my body to your mercies." The body is not actually his; it is merely his untigerish heart wrapped in a player's hide. But though that might suggest a certain invulnerability and crafty concealment — sticks and stones breaking the players' bones but not the playwright's — it is actually a multiplication of pain receptors. "The players cannot keep counsel; they'll tell all." Whatever that temporary playwright Hamlet means by "all," he expresses here as well as in his more famous speech to the players something of the annoyance of all playwrights at the necessity of routing language and vision through the medium of the stage. For theatrically the king not only may but must go a progress through the guts of a beggar.[5]

5   I am being rather hard on drama, I suppose, but it seems to me that drama is very hard on poets, primarily because drama is a collaborative enterprise which, to be got right, seems to require an enormous amount of work, talent, and luck on the part of a lot of people over whom the poet-playwright has little control. And it is also a combustible art form, as all the performing arts are, in that each performance no sooner emerges into being than it forever disappears. Only the script remains. Poets beginning to work in the theater, however, do not write scripts; they write poems, Shakespeare included

Had Shakespeare wanted to suggest the poet's sacrifice of verbal autonomy when writing for the theater he could hardly have found a better myth to dramatize than that of Philomela, with which he was of course familiar in Arthur Golding's translation of Ovid's *Metamorphoses*. In his prefatory "Epistle" to the translation Golding betrays considerable anxiety to underscore Ovid's "dark Philosophie" and high moral purpose, which if not immediately apparent in tales of nubile nymphs and light-hoofed satyrs becomes visible under close allegorical scrutiny. Wearing Golding's tropological spectacles, Shakespeare would have discovered that the story of Philomela illustrates the fact that "distresse doth drive a man to looke about/ And seeke all corners of his wits, what way to wind him out." [6] However, since Philomela's problem is linguistic and is solved by "art" — her weaving into the "warp of white upon a frame of Thracia" the purple lettering that indicts Tereus — we might expect Shakespeare to have seen in the tale not so much Golding's platitude about necessity mothering invention as the more specific literary problem of embodying thought in language and language in expressive forms, the problem that becomes particularly aggravating to the poet turned playwright and forced to deal in forms that must, initially at any rate, impede rather than enhance expression. If it is the artistic aspects of Philomela's plight that interest Shakespeare, than we might expect these to be reflected in the plight of Lavinia, the Philomela-substitute in the play.

Philomela's métier may have been weaving, but Shakespeare

(though less included no doubt than most poet-playwrights). Poems are to be recited, as many of Shakespeare's early speeches are, whereas scripts are to be enacted; and this apprenticeship in writing scripts and gradually abandoning the writing of dramatic poems must necessarily be frustrating, as I think *Titus Andronicus* indicates. Of course the "beggarly" aspects of the theater were especially prominent in the Elizabethan-Jacobean period owing to the amount of Puritan abuse directed its way.

6 Golding refers to Philomela's ingenuity, one assumes, though "man" and the masculine pronouns suggest that there may be something to be said in lecherous behalf of Tereus's ingenuity also. See *Shakespeare's Ovid: Arthur Golding's Translation of the Metamorphoses*, ed. W. H. D. Rouse (New York, 1966), p. 4.

repeatedly associates Lavinia with poetry, as for instance when Titus reminds the young Lucius that

> Cornelia never with more care
> Read to her sons than she hath read to thee
> Sweet poetry and Tully's Orator.
>
> (4.1.12–14)

Not only do poets speak through her, but her own tongue is given to melodic, lyric speech — or once was, Marcus reflects:

> O, that delightful engine of her thoughts,
> That blabbed them with such pleasing eloquence,
> Is torn from forth that pretty hollow cage,
> Where, like a sweet melodious bird, it sung
> Sweet varied notes, enchanting every ear!
>
> (3.1.82–86)

Marcus is equally impressed by the musical expressiveness of Lavinia's hands:

> O, had the monster seen those lily hands
> Tremble, like aspen-leaves, upon a lute
> And make the silken strings delight to kiss them,
> He would not then have touched them for his life!
>
> (2.4.44–47)

In the lines immediately following these, Shakespeare combines the eloquence of the hands trembling on a lute and that of the tongue whose varied notes enchant every ear into the figure of that first and greatest of all lyric poets, the Thracian Orpheus:

> Or, had he heard the heavenly harmony
> Which that sweet tongue hath made,
> He would have dropped his knife, and fell asleep
> As Cerberus at the Thracian poet's feet.
>
> (2.4.48–51)

This is a curious equation — Lavinia, demure and lovely, a most domestic lyricist compared to the wide-wandering Orpheus, tamer of beasts, free spirit whose art is his passport even to Hades and back. Yet there is a point at which their experiences coincide, a moment for each of them when the harmonics of tongue and harp lose their

enchantment. In this metaphoric frame, the rape and mutilation of
Lavinia become analogous to the death of Orpheus, so vividly described in the opening lines of the eleventh book of Golding's Ovid:

> With blowing shalmes, and beating drummes, and bedlem
>   howling out,
> And clapping hands on every syde by Bacchus drunken rout,
> Did drowne the sownd of Orphyes harp.
>
> (Book 11, 17–19)

We might hesitate to read the Orpheus myth at this point as a eu-
hemeristic account of the progressive cultural killing off (by *spa-
ragmos*, or ritual dismemberment) of early Greek lyric poetry by
Dionysiac ritual drama; but it seems unlikely that Shakespeare
could have read such a passage without reflecting on the fate of the
poet in the theater, where the melodies of his harp must submit to
being "clapper-clawed with the palmes of the vulgar" (preface to
Troilus and Cressida). From the expressive freedom of wandering
Orpheus to the squalid confines of the Theatre in Shoreditch: what
a verbal lopping off was there!

What I am suggesting is that *Titus Andronicus* metadramatically presents us with a rape of language, with the mutilation that
the poet's "tongue" suffers when forced to submit to the rude demands of the theater. The major image of this barbarizing of language by the theater is of course the rape and mutilation of Lavinia
by the Goth brothers. "Barbarizing" is an apt term here because in
the Renaissance "Goth" and "barbarity" are virtually synonyms —
and the word "barbarous" appears more often in *Titus* than in any
other of Shakespeare's plays ("barbarous Tamora," "barbarous
Moor," "barbarous, beastly villains," etc.). Moreover, the word
"barbarian" — as Shakespeare suggests when he has Marcus admon-
ish the ireful Titus "Thou art a Roman, be not barbarous" (1.1.378)
— once meant anyone who did not speak Greek or (later on) Latin
and whose speech therefore sounded like "bar-bar-bar" according
to Herodotus. So it is appropriate that Lavinia of the melodic
speech be assaulted by the Goths, who have been advised by the
equally barbarous Aaron to "strike her home by force, if not by
words" (2.1.118).

Lavinia's rape follows naturally from the fact that Rome has itself become barbaric. As Tamora says after her marriage to Saturninus, "Titus, I am incorporate in Rome" (1.1.462). With the nonlanguage of barbarism in the ascendant, the play abounds in images of linguistic distress, corruption, and mutilation. The suppression of civilized speech is given scenic emphasis when Lavinia is assaulted not in Rome (for the palace, Aaron warns, is "full of tongues, of eyes, and ears") but in the deep woods that are "ruthless, dreadful, deaf, and dull" (2.1.127–128). Even before the physical mutilation Lavinia's tongue is silenced. When she pleads for mercy Tamora cries "I will not hear her speak" (2.3.137), and when she pleads further Chiron interrupts with "Nay, then I'll stop your mouth."

Stopping people's mouths in one fashion or another becomes a major occupation. After the discovery of Bassianus's body, Titus's mouth is stopped when he ventures his "word" as bail for his suspected sons:

> I vow
> They shall be ready at your Highness' will
> To answer their suspicion with their lives.
> SATURNINUS. Thou shalt not bail them . . .
> Let them not speak a word; the guilt is plain.
>
> (2.3.296–300)

Writing is similarly futile. "Write down thy mind," Chiron mocks Lavinia: "bewray thy meaning so,/ An if thy stumps will let thee play the scribe" (2.4.3–4). So too in the following scene when Titus, appealing to the authorities as they pass on to the scene of execution, lies down and says "For these, tribunes, in the dust I write/ My heart's deep langour and my soul's sad tears" (3.1.12–13). But as Lucius says:

> O noble father, you lament in vain.
> The tribunes hear you not; no man is by;
> And you recount your sorrows to a stone.
>
> (3.1.27–29)

Shakespeare may still have Orpheus in mind here, since Titus picks up the "stone" cue and pursues the theme at length, the burden of his discourse being that stones are less hard than Roman hearts and in their silence less offensive than tribunes whose "tongues doom men to death." The Thracian poet whose song, as Golding puts it, drew "both stones and trees ageynst their kynds" would turn mute in Titus's gothicized Rome.

Thus when Marcus leads in the mutilated Lavinia, she and Titus are equally incapable of communication, she to speak, he to be heard. Reducing himself to her status as a form of sympathetic participation in misery seems to Titus an obvious response:

> Or shall we cut away our hands, like thine?
> Or shall we bite our tongues, and in dumb shows
> Pass the remainder of our hateful days?
>
> (3.1.130–132)

His suggestions take an interestingly theatrical form. A theater that truly killed Orpheus or mutilated the tongue of Lavinia might well become mere pantomime. Titus continues

> What shall we do? Let us that have our tongues
> Plot some device of further misery,
> To make us wondered at in time to come.
>
> (3.1.133–135)

In one sense it is not the Andronici but Shakespeare who plotted the "device of further misery" — namely *Titus Andronicus*, whose characters were being "wondered at" by an Elizabethan audience even as they spoke of the "time to come." What the Andronici ultimately plot is the last act of Shakespeare's play, a miniature Senecan revenge drama that has conferred "further misery" on everybody. But that is yet to come.

What comes immediately, busily plotting and acting in his own revenge drama, is Aaron, bringing news that the Emperor will release the two brothers in return for the hand of one of the Andronici. Since Titus's "word" would not serve as legal tender for the ransom of his sons, perhaps his hand, which he hastily severs, will. The transaction that finally takes place turns out to be a brutal parody of verbal communication, a "dialogue" of bodily parts in which a hand that cannot flourish is exchanged for two heads that cannot speak, all three returned to Titus by a "messenger." Without Lavinia's tongue, it seems, drama is rendered speechless or reduced to a sequence of sadistic acts.

In the absence of all civilized discourse, speech can only underwrite vengeance. So Titus ritualistically gathers his kinsmen about him —

> That I may turn me to each one of you
> And swear unto my soul to right your wrongs.
> The vow is made.   (3.1.278–280)

But though the vow to revenge is made, the hand that will execute it is severed. As the scene nears its end Titus, bustling about to do he knows not what, distributes heads and hands among his relatives, most notoriously to his daughter: "Lavinia, thou shalt be employed in these things! / Bear thou my hand, sweet wench, between thy teeth" (3.1.282–283). And bear it she does.

Perhaps more than anything else, Titus's insistence here on keeping Lavinia productively engaged ("Thrift, Horatio, thrift!") is responsible for the general reluctance to debit Shakespeare with the writing of the play. For surely nothing could better exemplify gratuitous grisliness of a most un-Shakespearean kind than the sight of the handless, tongueless Lavinia toting off her father's severed hand. The grisliness no doubt is gratuitous, a piece of theatrical sensationalism played for the "oh's" and "ah's" of an audience that evidently hungered for just such stuff; but it is also part of a dramatic metaphor whose consistent relevance to the nature of Shakespeare's play suggests that the author knows both what he is doing and what he is not doing. What he *ought* to be doing is implied by Hamlet's advice to the players about suiting the action to the word, the word to the action. Hamlet refers to acting of course, probably to a stylized form of acting in which verbal meanings are mimetically reinforced by gesture and posture, but his remark applies equally well to drama, which also depends on a coalescence of words and actions, poetry and performance, dead script and live actors. In Lavinia's rape and mutilation is figured the deflowering of the chaste poetic word, the private possession of the lyric-narrative poet, when it encounters the "barbarities" of the public theater and suffers the mauling of a raucous audience anxious for just such horrors as Lavinia's experience provides. Linguistic authority then passes into the possession of the Goths, and Titus's solicitations for his sons cannot elicit a merciful word. Titus's vow to revenge — the verbal promise that is to be redeemed by the vengeful act — implies Shakespeare's own sense of the necessity of finding a merger of language and action without the lyric Lavinia. But neither he nor Titus has found how to effect that merger, and the immediate emblem of this frustration is the useless hand of action being carried in the tongueless mouth of Lavinia. We arrive here at a grotesque parody of the proper union of word and deed in drama.

III

Drama becomes truly expressive through the marriage of the right language to the right actions.[7] In the theatrical world of *Titus Andronicus* Lavinia cannot survive, but with the loss of her melodious tongue the play threatens to dissolve into meaninglessness. Drama that tries to prevail by violent action alone delivers itself up to pure brutality without point or purpose. With the mutilation of Lavinia Rome degenerates into "a wilderness of tigers" whose medium of communication is not words but mangled bodies (3.1.54). Whatever meaning is to be found must be found in Lavinia if the play is to regain any sense of dramatic direction, and it is to her that Titus turns:

> Speechless complainer, I will learn thy thought;
> In thy dumb action will I be as perfect

7 This fusion of language and action comes about in different ways in different periods and in different playwrights, but it is usually considered ideally as a "marriage" and when it does not exist there is sure to be a manifesto commencing, as Antonin Artaud's does, "We cannot go on prostituting the idea of theater . . ." ("The Theater of Cruelty," in *The Theater and Its Double*, trans. Mary Caroline Richards, New York, 1958, p. 89). Thus Artaud goes on to say that "theater will not be given its specific powers of action until it is given its language," which is to be a total language of the theater, not just a literary language for the script. If Shakespeare felt in *Titus Andronicus* that his freedom of poetic expression was smothered by the theater, by drama as action, Artaud feels just the reverse, that the theater has been prostituted to the text.

As begging hermits in their holy prayers.
Thou shalt not sigh, nor hold thy stumps to heaven,
Nor wink, nor nod, nor kneel, nor make a sign,
But I of these will wrest an alphabet
And by still practice learn to know thy meaning.

(3.2.39–45)

Even action, which thus far has barbarized the play, could constitute a kind of language or expressive form if one only had the wit to find it out. In any event Lavinia's secrets must be discovered before any meaningful action can occur. The manner of their discovery — her turning the pages of Ovid's *Metamorphoses* to the tale of Philomela — is curiously relevant since the Philomela myth is not merely analogous to but a model for her own experience. In fact Ovid is a model for nature as well: the forest that so silently collaborated in Lavinia's violation was, as Titus says, "Patterned by that the poet here describes,/ By nature made for murders and for rapes" (4.1.57–58).

The stress on literary models is entirely fitting. Lavinia's turning the pages of the *Metamorphoses* is an almost literal representation of Shakespeare's own technique of writing *Titus Andronicus*. Not only did he find Lavinia herself (as Philomela) in those pages, as she is doing within the play, but like her he found a mode of expression — a tongue, language, verbal style — which he has incorporated into *Titus Andronicus*, though not with eminent success.[8] For the verbal style has had to encounter, in theatrical action, a kind of opposition which Ovidian poetry was spared, and the conjunction of the two has produced a rape instead of a marriage.

The marriage is lacking from the play because, presumably, it is lacking in its author at this time. Unable to create an interplay of language and action — to write poetry from which acts freely issue and to envisage stage situations in which poetry is implicit, to write a dynamic language of words and to create a visual language of movements, gestures, and deeds — Shakespeare presents us with verbal

8 In "The Metamorphosis of Violence in *Titus Andronicus*," *Shakespeare Studies*, 10(1957):39–49, Eugene M. Waith provides an excellent analysis of Shakespeare's adoption of Ovidian techniques of style in the play.

design on one side and physical violence on the other. The verbal
design is primarily Ovidian, lush in imagery and conceit, full of ex-
pansive figuration but fatally indifferent to dramatic context. The
obvious example is Marcus's forty-seven lines of detached mytho-
logical and metaphorical doodling when he comes upon the de-
flowered, blood-spurting Lavinia. Shakespeare does the same thing
in his narrative poems. Tarquin, for instance, must stand over the
defenseless Lucrece, suspended in a glandular frenzy for about
eighty lines while she runs through the tropes of moral admonition.
But that is precisely the point; for the poem will abide the delay,
perhaps even gain from it a suspenseful appeal, because in the narrative mode all action is created entirely *by* the language, not in
conjunction with it as in drama. In *Titus* Shakespeare fails to mold
his verbal style to the contours of shifting dramatic occasions; and
as a result word and deed become dislocated and often grotesque
in their mutual isolation or come together with a disfiguring clash.

The Ovidian poet then can function neither freely nor effectively in the dramatic mode. Lavinia has found in Ovid a means of
expressing herself, but it is a less than ideal substitute for living
speech. Pointing out her Ovidian forerunner, Philomela tells
roughly what happened to her, but Ovid cannot help her say who
has played the role of Tereus. Identifying the barbarous brothers
requires a most barbaric mode of expression: writing in the sand
with a stick held between her teeth. The analogy to the trials of the
poet-turned-playwright may seem fetched in from afar, but it
remains consistent with the metadramatic theme sustained throughout the play. Such writing is not only rather tricky but highly
frustrating since the medium of the stage performance is as ephemeral, compared to the permanence of the printed pages of Ovid just
consulted, as the sand in which Lavinia writes. Shakespeare's interest in the analogy would account for Titus's concern to preserve a
three-word message ("*Stuprum*—Chiron—Demetrius") that would
not seem extravagantly difficult to remember:

> I will go get a leaf of brass
> And with a gad of steel will write these words,
> And lay it by. The angry northern wind

Will blow these sands, like Sibyl's leaves, abroad,
And where's our lesson, then?   (4.1.102–106)

Where, indeed? Where the first performances, if not the First Folio, of all Shakespeare's plays are.

If all this suggests the frustrations of the theatrical trade, still Lavinia's identifying the villains promises something by way of a solution to the word-deed dilemma. The teeth that hold the "pen" are after all the same teeth that held Titus's hand earlier in a dumb show of linguistic and actional disfigurement. Rendered useless in the absence of Lavinia's tongue, the hand of revenge is now empowered to act meaningfully. Unfortunately, the agent of action, Titus, has been drifting away from meaning for some time, his mind slipping into madness. Precisely when it appears that all the prerequisites to revenge have been fulfilled and a sense of direction restored to the plot, Titus spends the remainder of Act 4 futilely petitioning the authorities, including the gods, for justice. Thus the play returns to its earlier phase of arrested motion. This curious stress on clearing away all obstacles to dramatic advancement, only to have the play continue to mark time, raises some structural issues that merit looking into. There are after all precedents for such undeveloping developments.

IV

In the middle of *Titus Andronicus*, through most of the third and fourth acts, the mad hero is baffled by the problem of securing justice. In a similar case T. S. Eliot has argued that Hamlet's indecision is "a prolongation of the bafflement of his creator in the face of his artistic problem." [9] However it may be with Hamlet, Titus's bafflement can be seen to reflect not merely Shakespeare's artistic problem, but also his means of solving it. The artistic problem, I have been urging, is how to bring about the marriage of word and deed in drama, how to suit the action to the word and the word to the action, presumably without trampling on, let alone merely o'erstepping, the modesty of nature.

9   T. S. Eliot, "*Hamlet*," in *Selected Essays*, p. 125.

Confronted by an artistic problem a literary novice in the Renaissance would consider nothing more customary and logical than to seek guidance from classical authorities. And as modern texts like *Shakespeare's Plutarch*, *Shakespeare's Ovid*, and the ever-expanding *Narrative and Dramatic Sources of Shakespeare* indicate, Shakespeare especially finds it natural to turn to literary models — Plautus, Seneca, Ovid, Plutarch but also Lyly, Kyd, Greene, Marlowe, and perhaps Beaumont and Fletcher later on.[10] In *Titus Andronicus* no more obvious symbol of a reliance on classical authority could be found than Lavinia's discovery of a "voice" in Ovid's *Metamorphoses*, though as we have noted it is the wrong kind of voice for drama. However, Ovid is by no means the only classical authority relied on by Shakespeare in *Titus*. Equally in evidence is Seneca, from whom Shakespeare drew certain incidents (such as the sacrifice of Alarbus in Act 1), speeches (e.g., 1.1.150–156, from the *Troades*), Latin phrases (e.g., 2.1.133, 135, from *Hippolytus*), and especially the dramatic form of revenge tragedy as Englished by Kyd and others.

If we back off and consider the play structurally it divides into two major actions: the rape and mutilation of Lavinia in Act 2 and the Thyestean banquet in Act 5. The former action derives from Ovidian poetry, the latter from Senecan drama; the former presents us with an image of linguistic mutilation, the latter with a macabre act which revenges that mutilation. Separating the two is a period of poetic and dramatic frustration in which Lavinia cannot speak and, when she can, Titus cannot act. The principal emblem of this frustration has been the grotesque conjunction of Titus's mutilated hand and Lavinia's mutilated mouth.

Admittedly this puts an attractive symbolic face on a most unattractive piece of stage action; and we might well look on this interpretation of Lavinia's carrying off of Titus's hand with one auspicious and one dropping eye if Shakespeare had not supplied reinforcements for this interpretation elsewhere. But consider for

10 *Shakespeare's Plutarch*, ed. T. J. B. Spencer (Baltimore, 1964); *Narrative and Dramatic Sources of Shakespeare*, ed. Geoffrey Bullough (London and New York, 1957–).

instance the form which Titus's attempts at communication take in Act 4. He has three messages delivered. First he sends the Goth brothers "weapons wrapped about with lines" (4.2.26) — that is, a Latin quotation from Horace written on a scroll wrapped around daggers. In the following scene he has his relatives and friends shoot aloft arrows to which have been attached messages addressed to various gods. The only response to these is the appearance of the pigeon-carrier clown, whom Titus sends to Saturninus with a third message: "Sirrah, hast thou a knife? Come, let me see it./ Here, Marcus, fold it in the oration" (4.3.115–116). In each of these cases, carefully specified, there is a most literal suiting of the word to the action, or rather a most mechanical attempt to do so by shaping an instrument of verbal communication around a weapon of action. Each message fails to register: the Goth brothers do not understand Titus's quotation from Horace, the gods do not reply, and when the clown asks Saturninus "How much money must I have?" for delivering his message he is hauled off to be hanged. Titus is on the verge of a similar fate, Saturninus having been borne beyond the seamark of his patience by all this importuning, but is saved by the Lucius *ex machina* of a messenger entering with news that as "general of the Goths" Titus's son is en route to Rome "to do/ As much as ever Coriolanus did" (4.4.67–68). Here finally, in the form of potential violence, is a message the authorities will listen to.

The hiatus between the two major events of the play — the period during the third and fourth acts in which Titus seeks justice from various authorities — results from Shakespeare's own reliance on authority, specifically the form of Senecan revenge tragedy. For the most arbitrary yet inevitable feature of that form is the "delay," that is, an essentially static phase following the commission of the offense and preceding the scene of retribution which provides a natural climax to the play. Unlike other Senecan practitioners Shakespeare seems to have realized that the delay constitutes a conventional caesura between the revenger's usually ritualized "vow" to revenge and his final "act" of revenge. With this built-in separation of word and act the Senecan form structurally puts asunder those two cardinal elements of drama whose marriage the playwright seeks to negotiate, and so appears to defeat him in his principal task. However, it can also be said to assist him in performing that task since it guides him to the eventual fulfillment of the word by the act after a period of structurally authorized frustration. A consciousness of this paradox seems reflected in Shakespeare's having made the division between word and act—a division already implicit in the form—unusually prominent by having the offense be against Lavinia's "tongue" and by repeatedly symbolizing the word-act dilemma as the play gradually maneuvers toward the Senecan action that avenges her.

This reliance on the authority of a dramatic form becomes increasingly apparent as the final revenge approaches. When Titus next appears he is in his study preparing a script for revenge:

> what I mean to do
> See here in bloody lines I have set down,
> And what is written shall be executed.
>
> (5.2.13–15)

His opportunity to enact his revenge drama arises when the Goths unexpectedly show up at his house to perform a play of their own. Not so mad as he seems, Titus easily perceives the identities of the actors within their roles of Revenge, Rape, and Murder and out of the failure of their drama weaves the success of his own, being inspired as he says to "o'erreach them in their own devices" (5.2.143).

To overreach the Goths in their own devices, however, is to outbarbarize the barbarians, which is precisely what Shakespeare implies as Titus prepares for the banquet scene. Guided by the principle expressed by Atreus in Seneca's *Thyestes*, "A wrong is not revenged but by a worse wrong," Titus tells the Goth brothers "For worse than Philomel you used my daughter,/ And worse than Progne I will be revenged" (5.2.195–196), and in the same vein he later hopes his banquet will "prove/ More stern and bloody than the Centaurs' feast" (5.2.203–204). This emphasis on outdoing classical authority—Ovid, Seneca, Greek mythology—is especially apt because Titus is the one character in the play whose conduct is dominated by a sense of authority and tradition. As H. T. Price has noted, Titus's religion "is a firm and somewhat naive acceptance of the usages consecrated by tradition. He kills Alarbus not so much out of cruelty, but because the traditional rites of religion demand it. He makes Saturninus Emperor for much the same reason. Sacred tradition requires that the eldest son of the Emperor should succeed. He stabs his son Mutius in wrath but also as a soldier exacting that same obedience which is the rule of his own life." [11] And his petitions for justice have all been attempts, however bizarre, to appeal to the authority of either gods or state.

So it is in keeping with Titus's character that the first murder in the banquet scene should be sanctioned by classical authority; he carefully establishes beforehand that Virginius's murder of his daughter (referred to by Seneca in *Octavia*) will serve as

> A reason mighty, strong, and effectual;
> A pattern, precedent, and lively warrant
> For me, most wretched, to perform the like.
> Die, die, Lavinia, and thy shame with thee.
>
> (5.3.43–46)

It is also to the metadramatic point that when Tamora asks "Why hast thou slain thine only daughter thus?" Titus disclaims responsibility:

> Not I — 'Twas Chiron and Demetrius.
> They ravished her, and cut away her tongue;
> And they, 'twas they, that did her all this wrong.
>
> (5.3.56–58)

Only metaphorically can the Goths be said to have murdered Lavinia; but the effect of forcing the metaphor here is to equate Titus and the Goths and thus to underscore the barbarity of his action. "Thou art a Roman," he was admonished in Act 1, "be not barbarous." Such an easy distinction between Roman and barbarian is no longer available since the noble Roman has indeed "o'erreached them in their own devices."

Would this not suggest Shakespeare's awareness of artistic fail-

---

11   H. T. Price, "The Authorship of *Titus Andronicus*," *Journal of English and Germanic Philology*, 42 (1943):58.

ure in *Titus Andronicus* and his recognition of the reason for it? Relying as he so rigorously has upon the "pattern, precedent, and lively warrant" of Senecan revenge drama has led him to traffic in a kind of theatrical sensationalism as barbarous in its way as the Goths in theirs. Like Titus he has overreached his literary models in their own grisly devices, there being, as Eliot has said, "a wantonness, an irrelevance, about the crimes of which Seneca [even Kyd for that matter] would never have been guilty." [12] For instance, Eliot might have pointed out, the orgy of bloodshed released by Lavinia's death. Amid this climactic flurry of stage action — it is instructive how many stage directions must be interpolated to make texts of the play intelligible to a reader at this point — the words "do," "did," "done," and "deed" (not to mention the more violent actional terms) sound eight times in the space of nineteen lines. The dramatic medium, in short, is now very nearly pure physical action ungraced by language. And that should remind us that during all the elaborate preparations for the banquet the mute Lavinia has been moving dutifully about the stage carrying out Titus's bloody instructions, playing her silent part in an action as calculatedly sadistic as that by which she lost her tongue. So employed she provides us even before she is killed with a visual representation of the barbarizing of language in the theater. In turning to Senecan authorities for theatrical instruction Shakespeare no doubt hoped to find how to render art dramatically expressive, how in the broadest sense to coalesce word and act. What he seems conscious of having brought about, however, is a mutilation of words, ultimately a ruthless silencing of graceful speech, by sensational actions. The result, as Sonnet 66 has it, is "art made tongue-tied by authority."

V

In the final, post-banquet part of *Titus Andronicus* still another authority comes into incriminating focus. Before going on to that, however, I need to return to 5.1 and consider the role of Aaron in the metadramatic theme. For despite Titus's anxiety to learn the truth and revenge it home, the full truth escapes him, and he dies unaware that a greater villain than Tamora and sons is behind most of his misery. Since Aaron falls conveniently into Lucius's hands the truth denied Titus does not escape his son. Like Lavinia's, however, Aaron's secrets do not come forth easily. In fact a good deal of very curious negotiating is required between him and Lucius before Aaron will tell his story.

Lucius, it bears noting, is entirely Shakespeare's creation, being absent from all the conjectured sources of *Titus Andronicus*. Similarly, Aaron has an importance in this play not previously accorded him. In the chapbook prose version of the story, which may have been available to Shakespeare, Aaron "never emerges as an independent character; he remains, until his concluding confession, the instrument of the Queen." [13] In *Titus*, however, he is quite independent of Tamora. For instance when in 2.3 even she is taken with romantic urges Aaron has his mind dutifully fixed on business: his "deadly-standing eye," his deep silence, his melancholy looks, his hair that uncurls like an adder, "these," he assures those of us who may have shared Tamora's diagnostic uncertainty, "are no venereal signs." On the contrary: "Vengeance is in my heart, death in my hand,/ Blood and revenge are hammering in my head" (2.3.32ff). This is melanism more than merely skin-deep; and to balance the moral chromatics of the play Shakespeare has added to Aaron-the-black Lucius-the-light, who will become Rome's new emperor and political redeemer. But first he must come to terms with Aaron.

The negotiations between Lucius and Aaron in 5.1 seem designed in part to associate Aaron and Titus and to dissociate Lucius from both of them. Aaron, in return for Lucius's promise to spare his child, agrees to reveal certain crucial information; but he insists that Lucius's promise be validated by his belief in a god, "what god so e'er it be." Lucius at this point rather abruptly graduates from a pagan Roman to a Holy Roman while Aaron acquires some Protestant phraseology in saying

13 R. M. Sargent, quoted by Maxwell in "Introduction" to *Titus Andronicus*, p. xxxvi.

> for I know thou art religious,
> And hast a thing within thee called conscience,
> With twenty popish tricks and ceremonies
> Which I have seen thee careful to observe.
>
> (5.1.74–77)

Nevertheless Lucius abandons the Roman pantheon and swears, "Even by my God," to save the child. This sudden Christianizing of Lucius to prevent the sacrifice of a child ought to remind us of an earlier incongruity of character, Tamora's famous and wholly uncharacteristic remark to Titus when he felt "religiously" impelled to sacrifice her child Alarbus:

> Wilt thou draw near the nature of the gods?
> Draw near them then, in being merciful;
> Sweet mercy is nobility's true badge.
>
> (1.1.117–119)

But Titus was following harsher gods then, and Alarbus's body was carved and burned because of what Tamora aptly defined as Titus's "cruel, irreligious piety" (1.1.130). Extremes, as Coleridge was fond of saying, meet. Titus's irreligious piety becomes virtually identical to Aaron's irreligious villainy. Perhaps worse, because whereas the godless Aaron is now seeking to save his child's life Titus is preparing the Thyestean banquet in which, on the best authority, he will murder Lavinia. Clearly, if Lucius is to be Rome's redeemer he must season the Titus-Aaron principle of vengefulness with at least a degree of godlike mercy. His first response to the capture of Aaron and child is vengeful enough: "Hang him on this tree,/ And by his side his fruit of bastardy" (5.1.47–48). As a direct result of his confrontation with Aaron, however, Lucius is forced to discriminate between the guilty and the innocent and to perform an act of mercy that stands unique in the play.

Though all of this is good training for a future emperor, Shakespeare appears to have more in mind. For instance Aaron's confession, so carefully bargained for, has metadramatic overtones worth noting. What he has to say, he warns Lucius, will be far from pleasant:

For I must talk of murders, rapes, and massacres,
Acts of black night, abominable *deeds*,
Complots of mischief, treason, villainies,
Ruthful to hear, yet piteously *performed*.
And this shall all be buried in my death
Unless thou swear to me my child shall live.

(5.1.63–68)

So phrased, what he has to tell is less a story than a drama; and he himself becomes a kind of interior playwright who alone knows all the strands in the web of plot and motive. As becomes clearer in his long confessional speech (5.1.98–120), Aaron is the indispensable character on whose plots Shakespeare's own plot hinges. Of course one could say that about any important character in a play. However, Aaron is pointedly associated with the kind of plotting that produces not only revenges but revenge dramas. This becomes most explicit perhaps when Tamora, arriving exactly behind time as he had instructed her, flourishes Aaron's forged letter and proclaims:

Then all too late I bring this fatal writ,
The complot of this timeless tragedy.

(2.3.264–265)

Aaron is not merely a plotwright of timeless tragedies but a veritable Johannes factotum of the theater — actor, director, messenger, prop gatherer, prompter — the man who tutors the Goth brothers, plants the gold, writes the "fatal-plotted scroll," coaches Tamora how to perform, fetches Titus's sons and directs them to the guileful hole, skips off and back again with Saturninus, reveals the bag of gold, etc. And so he goes throughout the play. Yet despite his manifold manipulations and scurryings about, his real identity as controlling intelligence is effectively concealed from nearly everyone else. Late in the play then when he encounters Lucius, Aaron the master-plotter contains the secret of Shakespeare's play — a secret that is in danger of disappearing forever: "And this shall all be buried in my death/ Unless thou swear to me my child shall live" (5.1. 67–68).

From this standpoint what seems especially noteworthy about

the Aaron-Lucius transaction is that the "drama" Aaron is privy to can be rescued from oblivion only if the merciful word can be found and sworn to. It is much too late for Shakespeare's play to be redeemed by the language of mercy, but that mercy is what it lacks seems abundantly evident. Thus the drama Aaron reveals to Lucius is a drama of blood and he himself the "bloody mind" behind it, the matrix and guiding principle of revenge tragedy. What is most monstrous about him is his merciless unrepentance, so Lucius feels: "What, canst thou say all this and never blush?" — "Art thou not sorry for these heinous deeds?" Not in the least, Aaron assures him, receding beyond the range of recognizable humanity into the shadow world of Elizabethan demonism and absorbing en route something of Satan and the morality Vice and darkening even further into the Negro Moor stereotype that Peele's *The Battle of Alcazar*, with its fiendish Muly Hamet, had helped popularize. Not that Aaron has any monopoly on inhumanity or unfeeling; Shakespeare's entire play, M. C. Bradbrook says, "is a Senecal exercise; the horrors are all classical and quite unfelt, so that the violent tragedy is contradicted by the decorous imagery."[14] Despite all the rhetoric of grief, anguish, and horror, there is a sense in which the play, like Richard Crookback, has "neither pity, fear, nor love." Miss Bradbrook touches on that awkward conjunction of language and action, Ovid and Seneca, that produces in both characters and audience an emotional "alienation effect," a most inappropriate Brechtian *Verfremdung* in the presence of what ought to be and try hard to be harrowing experiences.

Aaron then is identified as the foul, murderous core of the play, as to be sure he must be if his meeting with Lucius is to serve as a point of dramatic and moral transformation in the play: Aaron the black plotter actuated by vengeance giving way to the fair Lucius, who will convert revenge tragedy into a political morality play in which Rome's recovery is framed by justice and mercy. Essential to such a transformation is the purging of the state, which means that as much evil as possible must be funneled into Aaron so

14 M. C. Bradbrook, *Themes and Conventions of Elizabethan Tragedy* (Cambridge, 1960), p. 98.

that Rome can be cleansed by his death. Shakespeare gets that task done by inflating Aaron into a symbol of motiveless malignity analogous to the allegorizing of Tamora and sons as Fury, Rapine, and Murder in the following scene (5.2).

But Aaron as we have seen is also associated with Titus. And it is significant that Shakespeare chooses this point — that is, before the Thyestean banquet — to introduce so arrestingly the concept of mercy. The effect is to cast doubt on the ethical propriety of revenge, or at least to bring before the audience a moral perspective that cannot help influencing its assessment of Titus's climactic revenges later in the act. Thus the play moves toward the elimination of evil (Tamora, sons, Saturninus) but also toward an exposure of the evil involved in that process itself.

VI

The Aaron-as-dramatist metaphor may suggest that in looking back over *Titus Andronicus* Shakespeare has himself come to feel a bit monstrous and Aaron-like. At any rate since the play moves on to the banquet scene in which Aaron is out-monstered by Titus it is not surprising that the post-banquet portion of that scene is the most stiffly self-conscious piece of casemaking in Shakespeare.

On the stage lie four bodies and the culinary remains of two others, a scene of carnage from which Marcus and Lucius try to dissociate themselves visually, by ascending to the balcony, before seeking to transcend it through verbal exoneration. The tone of their speeches is extravagantly defensive. After such a play, what forgiveness? Given the silent slaughtering actions just performed, any discourse would ring out about as persuasively as that of the Four Knights at the end of *Murder in the Cathedral.* Who even is entitled to speak? These issues come to focus in the quest for a "witness" to authenticate the "tale." Marcus begins the task of justification but then shies off:

> But if my frosty signs and chaps of age,
> Grave witnesses of true experience,
> Cannot induce you to attend my words . . .
>
> (5.3.77–79)

So Lucius takes up the story, gets led astray in identifying himself as Rome's sacrificial hero, and pulls up apologetically citing his credentials: "My scars can witness, dumb although they are,/ That my report is just and full of truth" (114–115). Marcus steps forth again and, in a kind of parodic inversion of comedies in which redemption is figured in a rediscovered child, points to Aaron's child as tangible proof of villainy elsewhere. The finger is really directed at Aaron, who as Marcus announces "Is alive in Titus' house,/ Damned as he is, to witness this is true" (123–124). Marcus's age, Lucius's scars, and finally Aaron the villain. That the false Aaron should be the last witness for the truth of the story is ironically fitting since it is to him, "chief architect and plotter of these woes," that Shakespeare has largely entrusted the spinning out of his own plot.

There remains, however, one final and most important "witness" to be called in defense of the story, and it is to this witness that Shakespeare addresses himself in the latter half of 5.3. For the exoneration of the Andronici, so formally staged with risings aloft and speakings down, is a species of internal epilogue that in typical epilogue fashion makes a bid for the sympathy and forgiveness of the audience. The most immediate audience is the gathering of "sad-faced men, people and sons of Rome" (5.3.67), but beyond this audience are the equally sad-faced men, people and sons of London gathered in the Theatre at Shoreditch, not to mention generations of sad-faced critics. The metadramatic duplexity of address and audience, of Roman forum and English stage, is especially apparent in Marcus's appeal:

> Now have you heard the truth, what say you, Romans?
> Have we done aught amiss? Show us wherein,
> And from the place where you behold us pleading,
> The poor remainder of Andronici
> Will, hand in hand, all headlong hurl ourselves,
> And on the ragged stones beat forth our souls,
> And make a mutual closure of our house.
> Speak, Romans, speak; and if you say we shall,
> Lo, hand in hand, Lucius and I will fall.
>
> (5.3.128–136)

The lives of the Andronici and the theatrical life of Shakespeare's play are equally dependent on the judgment of their respective audiences, noble Romans and penny knaves. When Aemilius replies to Marcus thus

> Come, come, thou reverend man of Rome,
> And bring our Emperor gently in thy hand,
> Lucius our Emperor; for well I know
> The common voice do cry it shall be so
>
> (5.3.137–140)

the speech looks less like a confident forecasting of approval among the English audience than a somewhat anxious attempt to coach such a response from within the play. Surely the English audience is encouraged to participate inwardly in, perhaps to subvocalize, the "common voicing" of "ALL" in the next line:

> ALL. Lucius, all hail, Rome's royal Emperor!

My suggesting that Shakespeare here submits the life of his play to the judgment of his audience in the Theatre seems to contradict my earlier claim that it is precisely the theatrical milieu, including the audience, that debases the poet turned playwright. However, just as the Thyestean banquet scene revealed how the poet could become inarticulate by relying on classical authority, this address to the audience now suggests, perhaps a bit cynically, how the poet may become equally inarticulate through the theatrical necessity of securing the approval of the "common voice," which is no less corruptive than Seneca. That is, the play is based on one authority and directed to another. In fact the two authorities combine in that the classical Senecan features of the play come not exclusively from Seneca but from a popular English Senecan tradition. Thus H. T. Price notes that, while the play's classical pretensions are obvious, "it must not be forgotten that *Titus* imitates *every* sort of stage-trick that had proved attractive." [15] Simultaneously classical and popular, it suffers from both, as Shakespeare seems aware.

15   Price, "The Authorship of *Titus Andronicus*," p. 56.

Consider for instance the irony in the appeal to the audience and in what happens afterward. Lucius, forgiven by *his* audience and indeed so thoroughly endorsed by it that he is elevated to emperor, thus becoming official spokesman of the common voice, pauses for a final elegiac moment over the body of Titus, and then with considerable executive efficiency sentences Aaron to a breast-deep burial alive and orders the body of Tamora to be cast forth to scavenging birds and animals. Despite the mercy shown Aaron's child, ruthlessness reasserts itself, fully authorized by the common voice that cried Lucius into authority. Mercy is outlawed entire: "If any one relieves or pities [Aaron],/ For the offence he dies. This is our doom" (5.3.181–182). And as for Tamora — "being dead, let birds on her take pity" (5.3.200). With the popular voice behind him, Lucius is as unrelenting as Aaron. The voice of the lyric is nowhere heard in this desert; the Orphic artist must of necessity be sacrificed to the vulgar. In fact if Shakespeare's audience bestows grace on this play, as we know it repeatedly did in his time, that is because its desire for sensational and sadistic brutality has been catered to by a playwright who must bid for mercy by being cruel.

At the end Aaron and Lucius hold the stage, the latter capable only of the language of repellent justice — the "sentence" that kills by torture — and the former suppressing words that sue for grace in favor of his own brand of speech: "Ah, why should wrath be mute and fury dumb?" (5.3.184). Neither has been; only the voice of Lavinia has been permanently stilled. "If one good deed in all my life I did,/ I do repent it from my very soul" (5.3.189–190). There seems no need for Aaron or the play to repent on that score, since in both of them "bad" words and "bad" deeds have abounded. In that perverted form the play has suited the action to the word, the word to the action, after all. But at the same time it has created a coherent metadramatic theme, a mode of autistic meaning in which Shakespeare has played, for the most part ironically, on the goals and frustrations and the sense of loss of the poet exploring the complexities of drama.

POSTSCRIPT

As a postscript to an unorthodox reading, let me add (if only to afford God's plenty — that is, something to offend everybody) a historical note. In 1592 the Countess of Pembroke, as part of her effort to reform the English drama along the lines of complaint laid down by her brother Sir Philip Sidney in his *Defence of Poesie*, published her translation of Robert Garnier's *Marc-Antoine*. Garnier founded the French school of Senecan drama, in which all the brutal stage action is etherealized into a kind of radio-play eloquence. The redoubtable Countess even persuaded Kyd to recant and translate one of Garnier's plays, which became in 1594 *Cornelia*, all oratory and choral lamentation, the only action being that of a messenger slipping onstage to announce an offstage suicide. Then in 1594 Daniel dedicated to the Countess of Pembroke his *Cleopatra*, which was equally devoted to lyric and reflective dialogue at the expense of action.

Thus we have a semiofficial movement against the vulgarity of the popular theater with its stage sensationalism, a movement of genteel poetry against gross action, of classical propriety against popular demand. Surely the Shakespeare who wrote the epigraph and dedicatory note to *Venus and Adonis* felt some sympathy with this view. But the other Shakespeare, who was an actor and man of the theater, must also have realized the futility of such a position, which in seeking to purify drama could only result in sterilizing it, causing the theater to dwindle into the study. *Titus Andronicus*, which I think probably appeared while this Pembrokean movement was in full swing, offers abundant evidence of his being torn between two opposed "authorities," one demanding poetry and rhetoric like that of the Pembroke circle, the other violent action and spectacle. From this perspective Lavinia would become a symbol of the rhetorical closet drama so incompatible with the popular stage. To reinforce such a claim we might note that the only reference Shakespeare ever makes to a "Cornelia" is in *Titus*, where she is associated with Lavinia:

Ah, boy, Cornelia never with more care

Read to her sons than she hath read to thee
Sweet poetry and Tully's Orator.

$$(4.1.12–14)$$

This cluster of "Cornelia-sweet poetry-Cicero" seems especially noteworthy in light of Kyd's neoclassical *Cornelia*, which has a most oratorical Cicero for a major character along with its long-lamenting heroine. (There is also in *Titus* the "Cornelia" who acted as midwife for Aaron's and Tamora's child. Since she can inform on him, Aaron sends for her intending to kill her. Appropriately enough, she never appears onstage, being "silenced" in that great offstage Senecan void from which only messengers return.)

On the whole then the popular theater apparently gets the Shakespearean vote, as it obviously does in the long run, although in *Titus* he appears to acknowledge the high cost in artistic value that must be paid to the necessity of offering commercial appeal. At least part of the sense of revulsion in the play (as of a drama whose language stands fastidiously apart from its repellant actions) would seem to come from his unpleasant awareness of how far down one must write for this sort of success. Perhaps the fate of the clownish messenger Titus sends to Saturninus in 4.1 reflects a Shakespearean self-judgment of sorts. At any rate when the bearer of a communication in which words and actions are mechanically and ineffectively combined expects a cash reward and receives death instead, it is possible to infer a certain authorial uneasiness about the virtues of writing Senecan potboilers for the commercial theater.

III

Love's Labour's Lost

A DALLIANCE WITH LANGUAGE

IN *The Dyer's Hand* W. H. Auden begins a sequence of aphorisms and oracles with a quotation from Karl Kraus — "My language is the universal whore whom I have to make into a virgin" — on which he comments as follows:

> It is both the glory and the shame of poetry that its medium is not its private property, that a poet cannot invent his words and that words are products, not of nature, but of a human society which uses them for a thousand different purposes. In modern societies where language is continually being debased and reduced to nonspeech, the poet is in constant danger of having his ear corrupted, a danger to which the painter and the composer, whose media are their private property, are not exposed. On the other hand he is more protected than they from another modern peril, that of solipsist subjectivity; however esoteric a poem may be, the fact that all its words have meanings which can be looked up in a dictionary makes it testify to the existence of other people. Even the language of *Finnegans Wake* was not created by Joyce *ex nihilo*; a purely private verbal world is not possible.[1]

Auden's typically shrewd observations could be improved only by omitting the word "modern" since from the poet's perspective all

1   W. H. Auden, *The Dyer's Hand and Other Essays* (New York, 1962), p. 23.

societies bring a corruptive influence to bear on language and from society's perspective most poets must seem perversely given to solipsist subjectivity. There is scarcely a play of Shakespeare's that does not reflect its author's awareness of these issues, but *Love's Labour's Lost* is an especially happy hunting ground in which to explore the poet's relations to society and language. By its abundant indirections Shakespeare finds certain directions out; by indulging a sensuous enchantment with language he gives serious consideration to his medium, his art, and their relations to the social order.

Pursuing directions indirectly myself, let me pass from Auden to a story in the Los Angeles *Times* running alongside a photograph of a young man chopping at a fourteen-foot redwood stump. The story says that he is carving the stump into a statue representing a huge manlike creature called "Bigfoot" whom the Huppa Indians of Northern California claim to have sighted in the mountains for a number of years and in whose existence the young amateur sculptor passionately believes. What is interesting about this is that it so bluntly figures the artistic problem of achieving solidity and permanence in the art object. In this case the young man — no artist but a zoologist — seeks to reify his belief in Bigfoot by giving three-dimensional, iconic reinforcement to the vulnerably vague and (at this time anyhow, though the Bigfoot cult is on the increase) unprovable feeling that such abominable footmen exist. It is not enough to talk about such creatures; you must body them forth in tough and enduring forms, and the young man does so, if not in stone as one might expect, in redwood because in Northern California the indigenous symbol of temporal resistance is the Sequoia forest.

Redwood is tougher and more enduring not merely than human beliefs and feelings but than human flesh and bone, as the King of Navarre well knows:

> Let fame, that all hunt after in their lives,
> Live registered upon our brazen tombs
> And then grace us in the disgrace of death;
> When, spite of cormorant, devouring Time,
> The endeavour of this present breath may buy

> That honour which shall bate his scythe's keen edge
> And make us heirs of all eternity.
> Therefore, brave conquerors — for so you are,
> That war against your own affections
> And the huge army of the world's desires —
> Our late edict shall strongly stand in force.
> Navarre shall be the wonder of the world:
> Our court shall be a little Academe,
> Still and contemplative in living art.   (1.1.1–14)

"Fame," Milton tells us later, "is the spur that the clear spirit doth raise," which ought to remind us that the words "spirit," "breath," and "life" fall etymologically into one semantic cluster. The fame so sought after in brief life will achieve permanence as "registered" on "brazen tombs." This conversion of the evanescent into the enduring, though more indelible, is essentially the same as that in the Bigfoot example: belief translated into redwood statue equals human conduct and life translated into inscriptions in brass tombs. The translation of greatest moment to the poet, however, is not that of breath (life) into fame as registered on tombs but that of breath (words) into . . . what? What permanence or solidity can words have to match the registry of brass or even the bulk of Bigfoot in a redwood stump? How may "living art" — surely a more important matter to the poet than the Stoic *ars vivendi* or any more general art of living — avoid the temporal fate of all living things and remain "still"?

For unlike the painter or sculptor the poet works in a medium that is choice bait to cormorant devouring Time. Words to be sure have a kind of solidity as phonic objects whose existence depends on the shape and motion imparted to measurable masses of air. But in the mouths of that "human society which uses them for a thousand different purposes" words are primarily referential and therefore ephemeral, important not as substantive entities in their own right but as the windy agents of distant realities. From this popular standpoint Bacon's "first distemper of learning" is indeed "the study [of] words and not matter," a distemper into which the scholars of Navarre and most poets fall feverishly. Perhaps if the

revered Baconian "matter" were less drearily mute, if Bacon himself had not as part of his de-symbolizing program reduced the
"Book of Nature" to merely "nature," the errant scholars and
poets would be less in love with their disease. For the cure comes
hard, and not many can travel with the virtuosi of Swift's Grand
Academy of Lagado to the opposite extreme and abolish words entirely. It is they — Baconian empiricists, Royal Academicians, logical positivists — to whom Kraus's statement about virginizing the
universal whore of language really applies, not the poets. The poets
do not make language into a virgin again, they simply "make" her
— take her as a mistress with all her sins upon her and at the same
time re-create her. The others seek to purify language of the semantic sins she has accumulated in her wider social intercourse, to
make her virginally true and somewhat fastidious as well, shunning
coy ambiguities, puns, and paradoxes, averting her gaze from the
seductions of style. To bring "matter" into proper Baconian focus
the linguistic window must be polished to the point of invisibility.

Thus in both these roles, either as popular whore walking the
streets or as scientific virgin demure in the cloister, words as such
are diminished, wasting into insignificance in the very process of
becoming signs. From this oblivion of invisibility and general erosion the poet seeks to rescue words, and of them even more than of
mysterious W. H.'s he may say:

> And all in war with Time for love of you,
> As he takes from you, I engraft you new.
>
> (Sonnet 15)

But in this regard the poet has a great advantage over the dramatist,
for whereas the poet may carefully supervise the preservation of
his words in print (as Shakespeare did in *Venus and Adonis* and
The Rape of Lucrece), in the dramatist's medium of the stage his
words dissolve even as they are formed — dissolve and fall back into
the great public reservoir of language where he originally found
them and where they resume their referential status as signs. To
prevent this the dramatist may try to seize on words as his private
property, which means that he attempts to deny their public char-

acter as signs by depriving them of referential meaning. Of course
it is impossible to deprive words entirely of meaning. What the
dramatist can do though is to convert the usual transparency of
words into an opaqueness, transforming the clear window into a
stained-glass window so that words acquire in themselves an anti-
Baconian kind of matter.[2]

Giving a rich and patterned opacity to the clear window of
language is one thing Shakespeare is doing in *Love's Labour's Lost*.
It is not the only thing he does, and the ending of the play modifies
his doing of it very radically, but the doing deserves attention. In
perhaps no other play does language so nearly become an autonomous symbolic system whose value lies less in its relevance to reality than in its intrinsic fascination. The referential role of words
as pointers to ideas or things is consistently subordinated to their
relational role as pointers to other words. When Maria says of
Berowne "Not a word with him but a jest" the line has as its primary object the setting up of a syntactic pattern that in the rhetorical figure called "epanodos" can be turned inside out by Boyet's
reply, "And every jest but a word" (2.1.216). When Berowne says
"The King he is hunting the deer, I am coursing myself; they have
pitched a toil, I am toiling in a pitch — pitch that defiles – defile! a
foul word" (4.3.1–3), his speech is governed not by logic or conceptual intent but by purely verbal association. Such linguistic
doodling here and throughout the play reminds us that words, like

2 In "The Poet as Fool and Priest," *ELH*, 23 (December 1956) :279–298, Sigurd Burckhardt argues that such poetic devices as rhyme, meter, and metaphor have the major function of restoring to words "the corporeality which
a true medium needs." For a wider-ranging discussion of the spatializing of
the temporal in literature see Murray Krieger's "The Ekphrastic Principle
and the Still Movement of Poetry; or *Laokoön* Revisited" in his *The Play
and Place of Criticism* (Baltimore, 1967), pp. 105–128. The ekphrastic principle in literature is also discussed by Joseph Frank in "Spatial Form in Modern
Literature," *Sewanee Review*, 53 (Spring, Summer, Autumn 1945):221–240,
433–456, 643–653, and by Walter Ong in "A Dialectic of Aural and Objective
Correlatives," *Essays in Criticism*, 8 (1958):166–181; and it is of course implied
in the titles of such critical works as Cleanth Brooks's *The Well Wrought
Urn*, John Crowe Ransom's *The World's Body*, and W. K. Wimsatt's *The
Verbal Ikon*, to mention merely a few who stress the picturable aspects of
the voice while suggesting the speaking aspects of the picture. In the postscript to this chapter I quarrel a bit with Father Ong's excellent article.

poems, not only mean but are. They are for instance phonic erector sets, aggregations of sound which may be built onto to produce awesomely ramshackle structures like "honorificabilitudinitatibus" or dismantled and reduced to their basic elements, to the vowels and consonants that Moth wittily plays with (5.1.47–60) or to the single letters bandied between the Princess and Rosaline (5.2.38–45). The discrepancies between words as visual and as sonant objects may be revealed in the light of Holofernes's linguistic decorum — "such rackers of orthography, as to speak *dout*, fine, when he should say *doubt*; *det*, when he should pronounce *debt* — d, e, b, t, not d, e, t . . . This is abhominable — which he would call abbominable" (5.1.21–28). And for a verbal mercer like Berowne the stuff of speech has surface texture so that we find "Taffeta phrases, silken terms precise,/ Three-piled hyperboles [and] spruce affectation" contrasted with "russet yeas and honest kersey noes" (5.2. 406ff). But the major way in which *Love's Labour's Lost* bodies forth the physical character of language, promoting verbal matter at the expense of signified matter, is through its wanton use of the pun — since paronomasia no less than rhyme, rhythm, assonance, and alliteration exploits relations between words not as symbols of meaning but as sounds. In that sense it is amusingly appropriate that Dr. Johnson equated the pun with seductive physicality when he called it "the fatal Cleopatra for which [Shakespeare] lost the world and was content to lose it."

The aesthetic pleasure generated by all this linguistic fooling is "mirth," which in one of the play's dominant metaphors is begotten by the creative intercourse of language with wit. "My father's wit and my mother's tongue, assist me!" — Moth's epic invocation as he girds himself to deliver a definition in song establishes the gender of wit and language, whose issue is wholly verbal. Or to pursue this metaphor a bit, the creative act engaged in by wit and language may take the form of repartee in which the mutual thrust, parry, and riposte of words are associated with hunting, dancing, combat, and most of all the sexual act:

> BOYET. My lady goes to kill horns; but if thou marry,
> Hang me by the neck if horns that year miscarry.

Finely put on!

ROSALINE. Well, then I am the shooter.

BOYET.   And who is your deer?

ROSALINE. If we choose by the horns, yourself; come not near.

Finely put on, indeed!

MARIA. You still wrangle with her, Boyet, and she strikes at the brow.

BOYET. But she herself is hit lower. Have I hit her now?

ROSALINE. Shall I come upon thee with an old saying, that was a man when King Pepin of France was a little boy, as touching the hit it?

BOYET. So I may answer thee with one as old, that was a woman when Queen Guinever of Britain was a little wench, as touching the hit it.

ROSALINE. "Thou canst not hit it, hit it, hit it,
            Thou canst not hit it, my good man."

BOYET. "An I cannot, cannot, cannot,
         An I cannot, another can."

COSTARD. By my troth, most pleasant. How both did fit it!

                                                    (4.1.113–131)

The pleasure or mirth afforded Costard and the others here is delivered as a result of the procreative interaction of one person's language with another's wit, a kind of verbal copulation to which the elderly Boyet must be resigned in view of his "I cannot, cannot, cannot."

Berowne's generative potential both physically and verbally is greater than Boyet's, and the first full-length portrait we get of him exhibits his capacity for a kind of auto-conception involving the eye, wit, and language:

> Berowne they call him; but a merrier man
> Within the limit of becoming mirth
> I never spent an hour's talk withal.
> His eye *begets* occasion for his wit,
> For every object that the one doth catch
> The other turns to a mirth-moving jest
> Which his fair tongue, conceit's expositor,
> *Delivers* in such apt and gracious words
> That aged ears play truant at his tales

> And younger hearings are quite ravished,
> So sweet and voluble is his discourse.
>
> (2.1.66–76)

Even Holofernes can revel in the procreative power of his wit:

> This is a gift that I have, simple, simple — a foolish extravagant spirit full of forms, figures, shapes, objects, ideas, apprehensions, motions, revolutions. These are begot in the ventricle of memory, nourished in the womb of pia mater, and delivered upon the mellowing of occasion. But the gift is good in those in whom it is acute, and I am thankful for it.   (4.2.67–74)

And if the lowly Dull lacks wit and language unlike the devoted academicians it is because, as Sir Nathaniel says —

> Sir, he hath never fed of the dainties that are bred in a book;
> he hath not eat paper, as it were; he hath not drunk ink; his intellect is not replenished; he is only an animal, only sensible in the duller parts;
> And such barren plants are set before us that we thankful should be,
> Which we of taste and feeling are, for those parts that do fructify in us more than he.   (4.2.24–30)

Having no father wit and no mother tongue Dull must of necessity be barren. According to the Princess, however, even the "fructifying wits" are barren, for when she first hears of their characteristic mockery and wordplay she says "Such short-lived wits do wither as they grow" (2.1.54). With its paradox of withering growth her statement helps bring out the basic comment which the procreative metaphor I've been tracing makes on the conduct of the scholars. The intercourse between wit and words to which all their energies are devoted is ambiguous in value and effect. On the one hand it is procreative and vital, generating through mirth and amusement a community of feeling that goes at least partway toward binding society together. But on the other hand it is as barren as Dull's intellect because what could be a genuine union of words and thoughts, language and reality, has in their practice degenerated to mere verbal promiscuity, to a splendid but ephemeral dalliance between wit and words. Such a relationship is fitting

enough in a world of holiday and festive release. But in the world
of everyday toward which the drama moves, license whether verbal or sexual must give way to the governing forms of social order,
promiscuity to marriage. The final attitude which the play takes
toward this dalliance of wit and language is suggested in its own
punning title, for when words do duty for realities love's labor is
truly without issue and in the metadramatics of the play literary
form miscarries. But that is to get ahead of the story.

II

So one of the things this play does is to give words the function not so much of expressing the truth of things or thoughts but
of eliciting — through puns, metaphors, rhyme, alliteration, coinage, through all the devices that suggest the substantiality of language — verbal relations that are in themselves aesthetically pleas-
ing. But if Shakespeare runs with the hares of playful speech, he
hunts with the hounds of satiric sense as well. In fact most critics
have found it easy to regard the hares as existing only to be coursed
by the hounds. If so, Shakespeare lines up with the verbal skeptics
as a kind of "exteriorized" Berowne feeding the wormwood of
burlesque to the linguistic ills of his time — gongorism, preciosity,
pedantry, inkhornism, and plain ignorance. As satirist of verbal affectation and related abuses he would presumably aim to purify
language, to transform the whore back into a virgin. Thus aggrandizing words as substantive entities and satirizing verbal affectation
appear as twin aspects of the same desire, which is to convert the
public and corrupt medium into his private and pure property, giving to transient breath a solidity in which he can carve his own enduring shapes.

The impulse to take language for one's own is most obviously
figured in the opening scene of the play. To achieve eternal fame
in the mouths of men the scholars create a private society by verbal
fiat. They bind themselves to one another by giving their words or
oaths to each other, they bind themselves to the words of the statutes that define their obligations, and they bind themselves to the
study of words. As a result the court "shall be a little Academe,/

Still and contemplative in living art" — a transfixed (still) rather than enduring (still) social unit the central feature of which is its prohibition of women. Since this academe is verbally created its integrity is primarily verbal and must be verbally guaranteed. Therefore "no woman shall come within a mile of [the] court . . . On pain of losing her tongue" (1.1.119–125), and in the only other item revealed to us from the statutes "If any man be seen to talk with a woman within the term of three years, he shall endure such public shame as the rest of the court can possibly devise" (1.1.130–133). Figured in the oaths and statutes the interdependence of language and the social order is complete; neither can exist apart from the other. Even to say that the breakdown of language precipitates the breakdown of the social order is to imply a division between the two that is simply not there. When the scholars one by one break their words, that does not *cause* their private masculine community to disintegrate; it *is* that disintegration.

The major reason for the collapse of the academic society is that the language that created it in the first place was disjoined from the truth of human nature, which is defined in the phrase of that minor lexicographer and master lover Costard — "such is the simplicity of man to hearken after the flesh" (1.1.219). In the verbal world of academe the word has been set against the word — "will" as moral resolve against "will" as passion and the affections. The brave conquerors who "war against [their] own affections/ And the huge army of the world's desires" place passion under the lock and key of verbal oaths, subjecting will to will (1.1.8–10). The function of both Berowne and Costard in the opening scene is to point the fact that language so divorced from realities of human nature can achieve little more than merely verbal triumphs, let alone foster an enduring social order. Thus Berowne:

> Necessity will make us all forsworn
>   Three thousand times within this three years' space;
> For every man with his affects is born,
>   Not by might mastered but by special grace.
> If I break faith, this word shall speak for me —
> I am forsworn on "mere necessity."   (1.1.150–155)

Costard even more bluntly reveals the disjunction between language and truth. No sooner have the "deep oaths" been sworn than he "is taken with a wench" in the park and brought to justice. Forecasting the scholars' later devices, he first tries to evade the facts by quibbling with the language of the statutes:

> KING. It was proclaimed a year's imprisonment to be taken with a wench.
> COSTARD. I was taken with none, sir. I was taken with a damsel.
> KING. Well, it was proclaimed damsel.
> COSTARD. This was no damsel neither, sir. She was a virgin.
> KING. It is so varied too, for it was proclaimed virgin.
> COSTARD. If it were, I deny her virginity. I was taken with a maid.
> KING. This maid will not serve your turn, sir.
> COSTARD. This maid will serve my turn, sir.　　(1.1.289–301)

In the last line Costard abandons his attempt to evade the language of the statutes, which he has found is in its own way perfect, an absolutely closed system without verbal loopholes. But his last line underscores the fact that however perfect the system may be on its own grounds it is not grounded in reality; the word "maid" will not serve his turn by giving him a quibbling out, but the maid herself will "serve" him in the overworked sexual sense of the term. Thus when sentenced to a week on "bran and water" Costard can say to Berowne "I suffer for the truth, sir; for true it is I was taken with Jaquenetta, and Jaquenetta is a true girl" (1.1.313–314). In being taken with a true girl Costard has revealed himself a true man hearkening as true men do after the flesh. But separating these masculine and feminine truths and preventing their incorporation into the social order is a repressive language in the service of a repressive justice, or rather a language and a justice that are mutually defining, a sterile tautology from which there is no escape and into which reality cannot penetrate. So Costard suffers not only "for the truth," as he claims, but because the truth of human nature goes unreflected in the received language of Navarre.

At his humble level Costard acts as a weathervane pointing the way the dramatic winds blow. In demonstrating that language can neither substitute for nor suppress reality, that the victory of "will" over "will" is spuriously verbal, he exposes more than he himself understands. Not, however, more than the French ladies understand. At her first meeting with the King the Princess wittily gives point to what Costard has unwittingly demonstrated — the tenuousness of the bondage of will to will:

> KING. You shall be welcome, madam, to my court.
> PRINCESS. I will be welcome then. Conduct me thither.
> KING. Hear me, dear lady, I have sworn an oath.
> PRINCESS. Our Lady help my lord. He'll be forsworn!
> KING. Not for the world, fair madam, by my will.
> PRINCESS. Why, will shall break it — will and nothing else.[3]
>
> (2.1.94–100)

3 I suppose I should not overlook in "will" a possible pun on Shakespeare's own name, in which case the line "Why, will shall break it [the King's word]: will and nothing else" is a witty announcement of the puppetlike nature of the characters, so dominated by a transcendent Will.

"Will" is also opposed in this play to "grace." "Every man with his affects is born," Berowne says, "Not by might mastered but by special grace" (1.1.152–153). Given in Sidney's phrase an "infected will" man cannot rely entirely on himself, as the scholars try to do, but must enlist divine support to resist temptations. This theme might be associated with the frequent critical claim that Shakespeare is attacking Ralegh's circle (see Miss F. A. Yates's *A Study of "Love's Labour's Lost,"* vol. 5 in *Shakespeare Problems*, ed. A. W. Pollard and J. Dover Wilson (Cambridge, 1936). That is, Ralegh's "Schoole of Atheisme" — which Shakespeare presumably glances at in his "school of night" phrase (4.3.255) that combines "schoole of atheisme" with the title of Chapman's poem extolling studies, "Shadow of Night," and to which he apparently refers again in his phrase "base sale of *chapmen's* tongues" (2.1.16) — would, like the scholars in the play, deny "grace" (and women) and atheistically rely on "will" and study. But they are shown the error of their way, are obliged ultimately to confess (5.2.425ff) and to sue for grace to the ladies.

Considered linguistically the "will-grace" theme suggests that words, like men, have a transcendent dimension of being, especially for instance in the mouths of kings, priests, witches, and magicians. Can the poet in some way levy on this power to reinforce a medium all too liable to sublunar infection? The issue is only faintly touched on here, but it becomes prominent indeed in *Richard II.*

Considered dramatically "grace" is a condition into which play and playwright may be brought by a receptive audience. The play gradually associates the religious conception of grace with the romantic notion of redemption of the lover through the mercy of his lady. This kind of grace is withheld from these lovers: "Nor to their penned speech render we no grace" (5.2.147). At this point the ladies function as an interior audience refusing to grace the scholar-lovers' Muscovite production. The sequence then is from religious

The point here is not merely to reaffirm Shakespeare's much-noted verbal skepticism in *Love's Labour's Lost*. The skepticism is of course there, and the scholars are allowed to feed so fully of the dainties that are bred in a book and to inhale so deeply of fine phrases that they threaten to suffocate on syllables. But Shakespeare's treatment of the scholars suggests not a repudiation of the power of language but an acute awareness of its limits and of the comic consequences of exceeding them. The play has yet to establish a final attitude toward the use and abuse of speech.

III

Structurally the play divides into three phases — the formation of academe, the abandonment of academe, and a final peripeteia marked by the entrance of Mercade. The dominant theme of the first phase is the aggrandizement of words by the scholars, which makes its way against the abrasive sub-theme of Berowne's dubiety. This phase ends when the scholars' oaths and hence their closed society both collapse under the pressures of human nature. From their common fall emerges a new society formed under the aegis of disgrace but also built on a comic anagnorisis:

> BEROWNE. Sweet lords, sweet lovers, O let us embrace!
>   As true we are as flesh and blood can be.
> The sea will ebb and flow, heaven show his face,
>   Young blood doth not obey an old decree.
> We cannot cross the cause why we were born;
> Therefore of all hands must we be forsworn.
>
> (4.3.214–219)

During the second phase of the play the scholars switch from aggrandizing words to debasing them. Berowne having gone along with them in their ingenuous confidence in verbal power, they now go along with him in his comically cynical view of language:

grace to romantic grace to dramatic or theatrical grace, or more accurately, because of the scholars' dependence on will, from religious lack of grace (the Academe project) to romantic lack of grace (the wooing project) to theatrical lack of grace (*Love's Labour's Lost*). Sections V and VI of this chapter deal with the same issue from a complementary point of view.

KING. Then leave this chat and, good Berowne, now prove
    Our loving lawful and our faith not torn.
DUMAINE. Ay, marry there — some flattery for this evil.
LONGAVILLE. O some authority how to proceed —
    Some tricks, some quillets how to cheat the devil.
DUMAINE. Some salve for perjury.

(4.3.284–289)

To find flattery for this evil Berowne is most apt, and in his famous
exonerating speech he turns the word against the word with such
sophistical eloquence that perjury is transformed into charity:

> Then fools you were these women to forswear,
> Or keeping what is sworn you will prove fools.
> For wisdom's sake, a word that all men love,
> Or for love's sake, a word that loves all men,
> Or for men's sake, the authors of these women,
> Or women's sake, by whom we men are men,
> Let us once lose our oaths to find ourselves
> Or else we lose ourselves to keep our oaths.
> It is religion to be thus forsworn,
> For charity itself fulfils the law,
> And who can sever love from charity?

(4.3.355–365)

Berowne's entire speech, too long to quote, sums up the attitudes
expressed a bit earlier by all the scholars in their poem-letters to
the ladies. He pits language and vows against reality and nature and
concludes with Longaville that "Vows are but breath, and breath a
vapour is" (4.3.68).

Thus the scholars drift from one linguistic extreme to the
other. Having discovered that language cannot create *ex nihilo* an
enduring social order or legislate reality out of existence, they now
assume that words are quite without substance — mere breath. Like
Costard they have been taken with a wench, language, and like his
at first their defense is based on proving language a whore instead
of acknowledging themselves lechers. What they had set up with
all due formality as a marriage, they now prefer to annul and rede-
fine as a dalliance, demoting language from wife to mistress since in
one of the play's recurrent puns words are "light" — not only in the

sense of their being brilliantly insubstantial but in the sense of their being loose or promiscuous.

Such a view leads of course to verbal chaos. If words are merely appearances devoid of any intrinsic truth or power then one may do with them as he will. Oaths can be made and broken on the dictate of whimsy ("O who can give an oath?" Berowne cries — 4.3.250); facts are at the mercy of phrases; and meanings may be created, modified, or dismissed at will. In the dramatic worlds of chronicle and tragedy such a collapse of language generates or at least attends social and political collapse. In the comic world of *Love's Labour's Lost*, however, a built-in corrective in the form of the French ladies prevents the corruption of language from seriously impairing the social order. For despite their own very considerable talent for fooling in words the ladies have a greater respect for language than the scholars. Berowne's clever use of all his linguistic resources to invalidate the bonds of language and "prove [their] faith not torn" receives the hearty approval of the other scholars, but the comment which the play makes on his speech is supplied by the ladies, as when Maria remarks

> Folly in fools bears not so strong a note
> As foolery in the wise, when wit doth dote,
> Since all the power thereof it doth apply
> To prove by wit worth in simplicity.

$$(5.2.75-78)$$

And though the scholars, accusing language of false representation, are quick to annul their marriage to it, the ladies are equally quick to insist that the marriage be honored, that language whether intrinsically true or not can and should be kept true by conscientious usage. Thus when the King prepares to break his oath by inviting the ladies to enter the court, the Princess replies

> This field shall hold me, and so hold your vow.
> Nor God nor I delights in perjured men.
> KING. Rebuke me not for that which you provoke.
> The virtue of your eye must break my oath.
> PRINCESS. You nickname virtue — "vice" you should
>   have spoke,

For virtue's office never breaks men's troth.
  Now by my maiden honour, yet as pure
As the unsullied lily, I protest,
  A world of torments though I should endure,
I would not yield to be your house's guest;
  So much I hate a breaking cause to be
  Of heavenly oaths vowed with integrity.

(5.2.345–356)

The Princess's speech here calls attention to the dissolution of language that is corollary to the lords' assumption that words are mere breath. It also, in her insistence on fidelity to oaths, not only associates linguistic integrity with moral integrity but even suggests through references to God and heavenly oaths that language, like the moral order, has a transcendent dimension of meaning to which men must remain faithful. Most important though, her speech constitutes the redemption of the word by the word. Sworn on her "maiden honour" the Princess's vow not to enter the court intercepts the King's intention to break his own vow and thereby preserves his word. Shakespeare is doing here with words what he later does with deeds in both *Measure for Measure* and *All's Well That Ends Well*. In the "bed-trick" episodes of those plays Mariana and Helena substitute themselves for Isabella and Diana, thus transforming intended acts of lust by Angelo and Bertram into lawful acts of procreation between husband and wife. In this way the vows of marriage about to be abandoned are reaffirmed. Both language and marriage are rendered true as the word becomes united with its meaning in the act of wedded union. Much the same occurs in the present situation in *Love's Labour's Lost* as the King's promiscuous intentions toward his vow are countered by the Princess's vow and transformed into a genuine marriage between word and meaning. In a play as absorbed in language as this one it is fitting that redemption should take the form not of mercy or love, as it normally does in Shakespearean comedy, but of words themselves.[4]

4 This redemption of the word by the word seems especially significant because it occurs at the apparent expense of the comic form. That is, fidelity to

However, the redemption of language and of the scholars is far from complete. The fact that the King's word is kept true through outside assistance, the Princess's vow shoring up his original vow, reminds us that language is a public medium in which everyone has a stake. Surely the social order needs a true language no less than a true currency. In the marketplace of love — where seller, buyer, and money take the form of lover, beloved, and language — a valid linguistic currency must effectively unite what is meant with what is understood: love must be truly felt, truly expressed, and truly received. This paradigm for the dialogue of love is disregarded in *Love's Labour's Lost*, and love's labor is lost because the scholar-lovers cannot find the verbal *style* in which love can be genuinely expressed and hence genuinely received.

The style the scholar-lovers do adopt during the second phase of the play is that inflationary species of linguistic currency that was flooding the poetic market in the 1590s — the Petrarchan. "By heaven, I do love," Berowne says wonderingly, "and it hath taught me to rhyme and to be melancholy, and here is part of my rhyme and here my melancholy. Well, she hath one of my sonnets already. The clown bore it, the fool sent it, and the lady hath it" (4.3.12ff). A true enough translation of the communicative process of love truly felt, expressed, and received into a noncommunicative process involving fool, clown, and lady. The clown as messenger of love is an especially apt analogue to the Petrarchan mode, as we are shortly to see when the other scholars come individually forth to sigh their sonnets into the air while Berowne listens. With each

the oath at this point — and hence the maintenance of sexual distance between French ladies and Navarre scholars, the continued exclusion of the ladies from the park — involves a denial of the whole traditional movement of comedy from sterility and abstinence toward fecundity and marriage, the victory of life forces over death if we wax anthropological. Of course a period of alienation of the sexes, usually through the machinations of a heavy father figure, is entirely sanctioned by comic form; but what is unusual about *Love's Labour's Lost* is that Shakespeare not merely threatens to but ultimately does disappoint our generic expectations by introducing at the end of the play not the symbol of life and marriage, Hymen, but a figure of death and division, Mercade.

of the scholars reciting his sonnet for his own delectation it is clear
that language is now employed not to communicate love but to
celebrate it. Berowne's famous speech on love does not regard love
as a social phenomenon between man and woman but as a vivifying
inner event, an intensification of sensory powers:[5]

> It adds a precious seeing to the eye —
> A lover's eyes will gaze an eagle blind.
> A lover's ear will hear the lowest sound
> When the suspicious head of theft is stopped.
> Love's feeling is more soft and sensible
> Than are the tender horns of cockled snails;
> Love's tongue proves dainty Bacchus gross in taste.
>
> (4.3.333–339)

Exuberantly afflicted with love, holding their own emotional
pulses, and calling out their rising temperatures with gleeful woe,
the scholars have all become lyric poets singing the praises of their
malady less for the benefit of the ladies than for their own wonder
and delight. Compared to the pulsing reality of their overheated
blood, words have no apparent worth and hence can be lavished in
sonnets, declarations of love, flattery, and similar forms of conspicuous improvidence. From the kind of verbal hoarding represented
by their Academe project, the scholars have passed to the wildest
profligacy.

To the ladies, who advocate a stable currency backed by solid
gold reserves, the scholar-lovers look suspiciously prodigal and
their verbal coin counterfeit. "They do it but in mocking merri-
ment," the Princess says of their Muscovite wooing scheme, and
therefore "mock for mock is only my intent" (5.2.139–140). Of
the purely verbal nature of the scholars' courtship she remarks
"What are they/ That charge their breath against us?" (5.2.87–88).
And again:

> If they do speak our language, 'tis our will
> That some plain man recount their purposes.
>
> (5.2.175–176)

---

5 The point is mentioned by C. L. Barber — *Shakespeare's Festive Comedy*
(Princeton, N.J., 1959), p. 106 — who has written with grace and fine insight
on this play as well as the other early comedies.

The wooers lay out a great expense in words —

> BEROWNE. We number nothing that we spend for you;
>   Our duty is so rich, so infinite,
>   That we may do it still without accompt
>
> (5.2.198–200)

— but the ladies reject the proposed transaction, turning their backs on Moth's newly minted speech and sending them all away at last "dry-beaten with pure scoff." The ladies refuse to give audience to Moth's speech, and by disguising themselves they underscore the fact that the scholars' language is oriented more to the speaker than to the auditor anyhow. Whether in their role of pseudo-Muscovites or as themselves the scholars do not speak the ladies' language, and the crowning emblem of their verbal failure is their swearing new oaths to the wrong ladies:

> ROSALINE. But will you hear? The King is my love sworn.
> PRINCESS. And quick Berowne hath plighted faith to me.
> KATHERINE. And Longaville was for my service born.
> MARIA. Dumain is mine as sure as bark on tree.
>
> (5.2.282–285)

These new oaths ask to be compared to those in the opening act, for each marks a different form of linguistic abuse. The earlier oaths sought to bring about verbal purity in isolation from the larger social context. The later oaths are the product of a machine-tooled courtly style that parades words too easily and indiscriminately, setting the mask of "goddess of beauty" on dark-skinned Rosalines and blue-eyed Katherines alike. The contrast between the two kinds of oath, one in the service of verbal purity, the other in the service of verbal laxity, is paralleled at the sexual level in that the scholars pass from the self-centered celibacy of Academe to an equally self-centered "love" that bestows itself too readily and freely in all directions.

From the Muscovite episode onward the ladies manipulate events so that the scholars' love remains publicly unknown and un-acknowledged because the language in which they would express that love is devoted more to ostentation than to communication.

Thus when the ladies say they have assumed all along that the scholars were merely fooling, Dumaine protests "Our letters, madam, showed much more than jest," but Rosaline's reply emphasizes the gap between purport and understanding that the scholars' words have failed to bridge: "We did not quote them so" (5.2.794–796).

This underlying stress on language as a social instrument enabling, if the right words were found, subjective experiences like love to be shared by lover and beloved helps explain Rosaline's punishment of Berowne at the end of the play. The King is appropriately sentenced by the Princess to the sobering and comparatively wordless world of a "naked hermitage"; but Berowne is sent to jest in a hospital, to

> Visit the speechless sick and still converse
> With groaning wretches, and your task shall be
> With all the fierce endeavour of your wit
> To enforce the pained impotent to smile.
>
> (5.2.861–864)

For his infidelity to language Berowne must learn linguistic decorum, which decrees that words be framed not to his fancy as images of self-love but in accord with the feelings of his audience and the nature of the social, or in this case medical, situation. From his attempt to generate a communion of feeling between self and auditor under these trying circumstances will emerge his awareness of the nature and limits of language. Thus whereas he earlier said that he and the other scholars must lose their words to find themselves, he must now find the truth of words in order to find both himself and Rosaline. For not only do they, like the whole of the human community, have a share in language but through language of the right kind they may come to share one another.

V

I said earlier that *Love's Labour's Lost* turns its back on Baconian matter and absorbs itself in words alone, fashioning an autonomous verbal universe and playfully exploring its reaches. The impulse to construct a self-enclosed verbal context indifferent to outside realities and concerned less to communicate meanings than to exploit them autistically, let me call, with some apologies, lyric.[6] And remembering that at this time, around 1593–94, Shakespeare was also at work on the sonnets, we may see considerable evidence of a lyric impulse operating within and even against the dramatic framework of the play. For the evolution of action and plot is reduced to a series of verbal events: vows made and broken, games of wit and wordplay, penned speeches, songs, epistolary sonnets, and even "sentences" pronounced on the scholars by the ladies. Like Don Armado (and in part by creating him) Shakespeare "draweth out the thread of his verbosity finer than the staple of his argument." Thus the play seems almost an experiment in seeing how well language spun into intricate, ornate, but static patterns can substitute for the kinetic thrust of action in drama.[7]

The other major impulse in the play is the satiric: Shakespeare's burlesque of verbal affectation in general and of current linguistic and literary fashions in particular. Lyric seeks to appropriate words from the public structure of language and turn them into mirrors of the self. Its radical emphasis is on the isolated speaker whose words are not directed to an audience and hence are not so much heard as, in Mill's famous phrase, overheard. The epi-

6 With apologies because self-enclosed verbal contexts are hardly confined to lyric poems and because I may appear to deal a bit roughly with the lyric sometimes. The latter is true, but by "lyric" I do not mean actual lyric poems or the lyric genre in general but rather the lyric impulse when it gets imported, or more likely smuggled, into the domain of drama. Once in, it becomes colored by the particular shadings of the play in question – the lyric impulse in *Love's Labour's Lost* is a somewhat different thing from what it is in *Romeo and Juliet* – but in general it is associated with the insular, private, and indwelling, with the static and retarding, and with verbal purity.

7 In *Appreciations* (1889) Walter Pater said "The unity of the play is not so much the unity of a drama as that of a series of pictorial groups, in which the same figures reappear, in different combinations but on the same background. It is as if Shakespeare had intended to bind together, by some inventive conceit, the devices of an ancient tapestry and give voice to its figures" (London, 1907 edition, p. 163). This dissolving of the actional element of drama into tableaux, as Pater sees it, is equivalent on that side of the ledger to what I am stressing, the dissolving of the verbal element of drama into lyric states. In either case the kinetic is reduced to the static.

sode in Act 4 in which each of the scholars reads his love poem aloud while Berowne sits listening like a demigod in the sky is a perfect illustration of this aspect of lyric. Satire on the other hand turns language back on society, presumably in the interests of sanative castigation. Its radical emphasis therefore is less on the speaker than on the audience under attack. In *Love's Labour's Lost* two kinds of satire are distinguishable: that of the French ladies, which operates on the scholars with the aim of purging them of faults; and that of the scholars and especially Berowne, which, perhaps most obviously in their comments on the unworthiness of the Nine Worthies, functions destructively as a form of self-aggrandizing mockery, punitive rather than purgative.

Perhaps now I can work toward the metadramatic implications of all this. In the scholars we see a lyric appropriation of words, a desire to create through word power a world insulated against such outside realities as women and such inner realities as passion — "the huge army of the world's desires" and "your own affections" (1.1.9–10). Against this bubble of lyric seclusion is set the abrasive of the French ladies, the outer world of fact and substance which expresses itself in ridicule, demonstrating through "pure scoff" the futility of words divorced from the public body of language and used only as the kept mistress of private feeling. From this conflict emerges a view of language as a medium of social exchange in the most generous sense, a medium that is true to itself when it enables men and women to share the inner experience of love, thus becoming the verbal sacrament that confirms "the marriage of true minds." [8] As the characters move toward a recog-

8 It should be noted that Shakespeare here stresses the referential use of language — true words to convey true thoughts revealing true minds — and so seems to play down the ekphrastic quality or corporeality of speech to which so much of the play is devoted. The ladies, that is, ask words to serve as clear windows onto meaning. I think we need to accept this less as a final position at which Shakespeare has arrived than as a corrective to the verbal extravagances of the scholars, who have glorified words as substantive entities at the gross expense of words as symbolizing agents. Words indeed "are," as the bulk of this play dazzlingly demonstrates, but words also "mean," as the French ladies keep insisting. Shakespeare knows that without "being," or a physical structure, the meaning of language drifts inexpressibly free, unable to find a local habitation for human thought and feeling. And he knows too

nition of language not as an instrument of either private expression or public attack but as an agency of social communion, so the generic movement of the play itself proceeds through lyric and satire toward the comic vision that reconciles both. The comic form leads to the acceptance of the isolated individual (associated here with lyric) into a society purged of harshness and discord (or the satiric), a social integration for which the conventional symbol is the wedding. But of course in *Love's Labour's Lost* the wedding does not take place.

> Our wooing doth not end like an old play —
> Jack hath not Jill. These ladies' courtesy
> Might well have made our sport a comedy.
>   (5.2.884–886)

The threshold of comic fulfillment is reached but not crossed: it "wants a twelvemonth and a day/ And then 'twill end" (5.2.887–888). In the interval the truth of the feelings must be tested against the dissolvent of time and emerge pure if it is to be committed to a "world-without-end bargain." And in Berowne's case the wormwood of satire, the "mocks and wounding flouts,"

> Which you on all estates will execute
> That lie within the mercy of your wit,

must be weeded from his brain before he will have truly found both himself and the way to Rosaline.

Speculating about Shakespeare's stake in this is of course risky, but perhaps it is not too much to suggest that through his imaginative involvement in this play he has worked out some metaphoric formulations of the poet's responsibilities to his medium and his art. The poet must come to realize that he cannot transform language by force to serve his pleasure. He cannot try like the scholars to seize the Word and inflate it into a self-contained world in the

that without "meaning," or a symbolizing capacity, language becomes merely phonic stuff, an opaque structure of sound incapable of uniting men to the world or to each other. This duality of speech is nowhere so apparent as in poetry, which demands, as *Love's Labour's Lost* finally does, that both dimensions of the word be given their due. (See in this connection the postscript to this chapter.)

image of his own desires since that is to appropriate the Word to himself, and it does not belong to him. Seeking to virginize language for himself is as futile in the long run as the scholars' attempt to ensconce themselves in celibacy. If language is to serve the poet, he must serve her as well; and that means recognizing not only her generosity to him but also her independence from him. It means recognizing that language is like Nature in that she

> never lends
> The smallest scruple of her excellence
> But like a thrifty goddess she determines
> Herself the glory of a creditor,
> Both thanks and use.
>
> (*Measure for Measure*, 1.1.37–41)

The trouble with lyric celibacy is that it fails to acknowledge that it is taking words on loan and must return "both thanks and use" (that is, interest). The way the poet can return thanks and use to language and enrich her for her enrichment of him is by helping her fulfill her role as the bringer of social communion. In the best sense of liberality he must give in return.[9] The scholars, however,

9 The doctrine of liberality, which informs Shakespeare's notions of language, sexuality, and social exchange in general, is exhaustively and in fact interminably discussed by Seneca in the six books of his essay *De Beneficiis* (translated in 1578 by Arthur Golding as *Concerning Benefiting*) and more succinctly in his moral epistle "On Benefits." The importance of the doctrine is suggested by Seneca in what follows:

> What we need is a discussion of benefits and the rules for a practice that constitutes the chief bond of human society. We need to be given a law of conduct in order that we may not be inclined to thoughtless indulgence that masquerades as generosity, in order too that this very vigilance, while it tempers, may not check our liberality, of which there ought to be neither any lack nor any excess. We need to be taught to give willingly, to receive willingly, to return willingly, and to set before us the high aim of striving not merely to equal but to surpass in deed and spirit those who have placed us under obligation, for he who has a debt of gratitude to pay never catches up with the favor unless he outstrips it.
>
> (*On Benefits*, I.iv.2–3; p. 19, Loeb Classical Library edition, trans. John W. Bassore)

For a brilliant discussion of the iconological tradition concerning liberality from classical to Renaissance times see the chapter on "Seneca's Graces" in Edgar Wind's *Pagan Mysteries in the Renaissance* (New Haven, Conn., 1968).

pass from the non-giving of celibacy to the pseudo-giving (license in the guise of liberality) of a "love" that is made to look like promiscuity when they make their vows to the wrong ladies. Two extremes of sexual conduct correspond to two extremes of linguistic usage, and underlying both is an essential selfishness. Sexually both celibacy and promiscuity deny nature her due ("use"), which is children: if man owes God a death as Hal tells the sweating Falstaff at Shrewsbury, he owes Nature a child as the first seventeen of Shakespeare's sonnets repeatedly insist. And linguistically both verbal purity that aggrandizes words, as in Academe, and verbal prodigality that degrades them, as in the wooing sequences, deny language her due, which is, Shakespeare seems to feel in this play, the genuine marriage of word and meaning in drama.

For in drama the poet, far from using language selfishly, gives his words to actors who in turn give them to an audience. Instead of removing words from public circulation the dramatic poet allows them truly to become a medium of social exchange, circulating freely within the community of the theater, and indeed by virtue of this circulation *creating* a community of what were merely so many random individuals before the play began. That this or a similar realization is figured in *Love's Labour's Lost* is suggested in part by the fact that the play traces in its form the flow of the communicative sequence "speaker-language-audience," passing at the end from a stress on the speaking voice and the almost limitless resources of language available to it to a stress on the participatory role played by the audience. This is most succinctly rendered in Rosaline's rebuke of Berowne:

> A jest's prosperity lies in the ear
> Of him that hears it, never in the tongue
> Of him that makes it.
>
> (5.2.871–873)

"Tongue" as she uses it neatly combines both the voice of the speaker and his language, and her radical deemphasis of the two at this point is a fit corrective to Berowne's radical overemphasis of them earlier.

Nonetheless the play ends on an ellipsis of unfulfillment, and that obliges us to consider certain matters of dramatic form.[10] I began this reading with some remarks about the corporeality of language, which is represented in this play by the sacrifice of external matter, or referential meaning, to verbal matter, or words as substantive entities. In this way transient breath is given a solidity in which the poet can carve enduring shapes. And so he delightfully does, fashioning sonnets, songs, intramural patterns of linguistic play, puns within puns, rhyme on rhyme. Like the scholars of Academe or the lady of Shalott in her room, he withdraws into the hothouse of art shutting the window on the outside world where French ladies amusedly await and Lancelots ride singing "Tirra lirra." Of course no playwright, however insistent his lyric urges, ever completely shuts that window so long as his play goes before an audience. But perhaps the dramatic analogue to the lyric is the court play full of in-group jokes, obscure allusions, and sundry verbal cates for a select audience of aesthetes, a play that turns its back like the scholars on a wider audience.[11] From this standpoint the

10 In "Love's Labour's Lost," Shakespeare Quarterly, 4(1953):411–426 Anne Righter (writing under her maiden name, Bobbyann Roesen) first pointed out in detail that the basic contrast in the play is between art's illusions and reality; see also her briefer remarks in Shakespeare and the Idea of the Play (London, 1962), pp. 110–112. In Shakespeare and the Confines of Art (London, 1968) — a fine book which I ran across after first publishing my own notions about the play and after revising them in this chapter — Philip Edwards offers some excellent arguments against interpreting the play along moral lines and in favor of considering it metadramatically. The reversal at the end of the play, he insists, is not Shakespeare's way of indicating moral disapproval of his characters' attitudes toward love. "By a device of art, Shakespeare tries to subject the world of art to evaluation in terms external to that world. He behaves unfairly to the creatures of comedy, not because he thought them lacking in the sagacity and maturity he might expect of people in life, but because he wished, in a jest, to protest that a certain form of comedy was not capable of showing the vicissitudes of things. It is a formal and not a moral dissatisfaction that Shakespeare shows" (p. 48).

11 Love's Labour's Lost is clearly an esoteric play for private audiences. The first recorded performance was before Queen Elizabeth and her court during the Christmas season of 1597. For the Christmas revels of 1604 a private performance was given at either the Earl of Salisbury's or the Earl of Southampton's house. Richard David, the New Arden editor, guesses that it was

ending implies Shakespeare's rejection of the social narcissism of this kind of drama and his acceptance at least in theory of the more vital and variegated world of the public theaters.

From the standpoint of language Shakespeare appears to accept Berowne's remark about penned speeches, wooing in rhyme, taffeta phrases, etc.: "these summer-flies/ Have blown me full of maggot ostentation" (5.2.408–409). This verbal self-inflation of the lyric has undesirable side effects also on literary form. Lyric, which deals primarily in states of resolution, "is" whereas drama "does" or "acts." Acts inevitably generate other acts, re-actions, and as there is no end to the consequences of an act there is always an element of the arbitrary about the ending of a play (hence the quip about comedy ending with weddings because after that the tragedy begins). This is brought out forcefully when in response to the King's "Come, sir, it wants a twelvemonth and a day/ And then 'twill end" Berowne says "That's too long for a play" (5.2.887–888). The reason for this imaginative extension of the characters' experience a year and a day beyond the formal boundaries of the play is the act of dying reported by the messenger Mercade, an act whose consequences are too serious to be contained by the fragile frame of Shakespeare's art in *Love's Labour's Lost*.

This collapse of form through the sudden importation of acts and consequences is reflected within the play by other instances of aborted drama. First there is the Muscovite episode in which the scholars' masque-drama is repudiated by its audience of French ladies. "I see the trick on it" Berowne says afterward —

> here was a consent,
> Knowing aforehand of our merriment,
> To dash it like a Christmas comedy.
>
> (5.2.460–462)

Then there is the pageant of the Nine Worthies, which Berowne urges the King to permit because " 'tis some policy/ To have one show worse than the King's and his company" (5.2.513–514).

first performed in a private house at Christmas 1593 ("Introduction," p. li). The fact that it is an in-group play satirizing in-group behavior is in accord with its simultaneously capitalizing on and satirizing verbal affectation.

Masque and pageant are both pictured as types of "form confounded" when the Princess overrules the King's objections to staging the pageant:

> That sport best pleases that doth least know how,
> Where zeal strives to content and the contents
> Dies in the zeal of that which it presents.
> Their form confounded makes most form in mirth
> When great things labouring perish in their birth.
> BEROWNE. A right description of our sport, my lord.
>
> (5.2.517–522)

A right description of *Love's Labour's Lost* too, where despite the mirth it has begotten, the intercourse of wit and words has labored in vain to give birth to drama. And finally there is the performance of the pageant itself, which is left uncompleted when the dark figure of Mercade enters with news of the French king's death, after which Berowne says "Worthies, away! the scene begins to cloud" (5.2.730). Metadramatically the scene begins to cloud in Shakespeare's play no less than in that of the Worthies, since in both is "form confounded."

Both indeed have had non-forms to begin with. The pageant consists merely in the random entrance of each Worthy to announce his identity in ranting verse — Pompey, Alexander, Judas, Hercules, and Hector is as far as they get. No special sequence of entrances being required and no action occurring, the pageant is devoid of both form and plot. *Love's Labour's Lost* itself is no more devoid of plot than Falstaff is devoid of a backbone, but one must work through a lot of verbal suet to find it. If Shakespeare draweth out the thread of his verbosity finer than the staple of his argument, that is especially true when "argument" is construed in the sense of "plot." With plot and action submerged in tides of words *Love's Labour's Lost* becomes the reverse of *Titus Andronicus* where language and poetry are overwhelmed by barbaric actions and plots. Now not only is action minimized throughout the play but at the end the one action we are sure will occur — if not the wedding at least the bethrothal of the lovers — is rudely suppressed in favor of the year-long punishments. Here is a kind of mutilation and rape of comic form or plot inversely analogous to the mutilation of the poetic word in *Titus Andronicus.*

All of these breakdowns of non-form and interruptions of dramatic performances within the play reinforce the inconclusiveness of *Love's Labour's Lost* itself brought on by the fracturing of a static lyric framework. Perhaps this is implied in the final lines of the play: "The words of Mercury are harsh after the songs of Apollo." The prosaic "words" of Mercade-Mercury (both messengers, one of the gods, the other of death) return Shakespeare's play from the realm of art presided over by the god of lyric poetry, Apollo ("As sweet and musical/ As bright Apollo's lute" — 4.3.342–343), to the mortal world of everyday governed by time and death. And this shattering of the fragile shape of the play is analogous to the shattering of the scholars' "little Academe,/ Still and contemplative in living art."

Purely verbal self-containment cannot cordon art off from reality. It is not enough to carve isolated shapes in words — to solidify as Shakespeare has a line or couplet, a sequence of repartee, even a scene. The "songs of Apollo" are vulnerable to the harsh "words of Mercury" precisely because they are individually isolated units. If the "endeavour of this present breath" is to make its author one of the "heirs of all eternity" words themselves must be more than breath of the kind that can be blown away by messengers of mortality. The material solidity of words can be stressed by sheer linguistic play, but the result is not an enduring solidity. Linguistic play must graduate into dramatic play, and that involves the collusion of art and nature, language and action. Only when anchored within a context of action, deriving from it and contributing to it, are words finally safe from cormorant devouring Time.[12] *Love's Labour's Lost* embodies Shakespeare's discovery that drama is the literary form of true liberality and that drama achieves fulfillment when verbal celibacy and verbal prodigality give way to a genuine marriage of words to action.

With this marriage of words and actions within the play an

12   This discovery, arrived at by the route of failure in this play, is successfully incorporated into the structure of *Romeo and Juliet*, as I argue in the following chapter.

ideal "marriage of true minds" — the minds of poet, actors, and audience — is consummated in the Theatre itself. But it is especially in dramatic comedy where everyone is bound together in the festivity of the ending that the perfect imaginative and social union occurs. To achieve that union in *Love's Labour's Lost* would take, as Berowne says, "too long for a play"; and Shakespeare realizes full well that a "great feast of languages" will not serve as a substitute. But through the raising and purging of linguistic delight, he has perhaps come to realize how language in the service of the comic vision can create an image of social communion shared not only by the characters within but by the audience without as well. That achievement is not to be found here, but like the marriages it stands in the offing. It wants perhaps less than "a twelvemonth and a day" before *A Midsummer Night's Dream* capitalizes on the rich gains of *Love's Labour's Lost* to usher in the great train of Shakespearean comedy.

POSTSCRIPT

My emphasis in this and subsequent chapters on the objective dimension of literature might seem to conflict with the position of Walter F. Ong in his excellent article "A Dialectic of Aural and Objective Correlatives." [13] Father Ong, as I read him, is fearful that literature becomes dehumanized when critics allow spatial metaphors to acquire too much prominence in their treatment of works, when literature becomes likened to verbal ikons and well-wrought urns, speaking pictures, and other objects that betray a modern visualist bias of the sort lamented by Marshall McLuhan. Against sight therefore Father Ong pits sound, against the objective, the aural: "All verbalization, including all literature, is radically a cry, a sound emitted from the interior of a person. . . ." This "interiority" possessed by sound, Father Ong feels, gives rise to the personal, distinctively human quality of literature, provided we think of literary works not as verbal artifices shaped in space (Aristotle's *poiêses*) but as voiced expressions.

One might argue that Father Ong casts an essentially lyric def-

13 See footnote 2 above.

inition over all literature and that of all literary forms drama is least well defined as "a cry, a sound emitted from the interior of a person." Drama is a medley of displaced, projected, disguised voices orchestrated by an invisible conductor, and though we may hypothesize an "interior" for Iago and Hamlet and Prospero on the basis of what they say, the voice of Shakespeare is nowhere to be heard. Of course even the lyric poet is a caster of voices, a ventriloquist, and to that extent a depersonalizer of his art. On the other hand it is surely true that literature seeks to invest the written word with the distinctiveness of "voice," to personalize language by crafting a style in which we hear the pitch and phrasing, the rhythm, intonation, and pace of human utterance, though not the direct utterance of individual authors.

Nevertheless in imparting to words the personal signature of voice the poet relies heavily on their sonant features, their objective properties, rather than reducing words to the status merely of semantic carriers.[14] It is precisely when that reduction is made, as in scientific language, especially mathematics, that the quality of personal voice in symbols is lost. (As visually we look through the objective features of mathematical symbols — invisible windows offering us access to their referents — so from an aural standpoint we hear through them. They are sounds issued in a monotone, with perfectly regular cadence as though by a metronome afflicted with an urge to communicate.) The interiority of voice that Father Ong admires derives largely from the objective dimension of speech he prefers to minimize — from sound conceived of not merely as measurable wavelengths but as shaped noise (hence no longer noise), all its objective constituents having been seduced into a gestalt that is distinctively human.

In ordinary language objects in the world become fully realized or subjectively available to us in our acts of naming them; and subjectivity becomes realized — reflection is made available to us and ourselves knowable — when objectified in words. In literary language this fusion of the subjective and objective is complete. Father Ong uses as epigraph to his article the eagle's remark to the

14   See in this connection footnote 8 above.

passenger-Chaucer as he carries him upward to the house of Fame
— "Soun ys noght but air ybroken." [15] No doubt Chaucer the poet
had his tongue in his cheek, knowing full well as Father Ong says
that "this simple reduction of sound to 'broken' air and thus to spatial components was psychologically unreal, much too facile." But
even "ybroken" air can have a certain material massiveness to it.
Don't you hear it? the eagle asks Chaucer as they approach Fame's
windy mansion:

> "What?" quod I. "The grete soun,"
> Quod he, "that rumbleth up and down
> In Fames Hous, ful of tydynges,
> Bothe of feir speche and chydynges,
> And of fals and soth compouned:
> Herke wel, hyt is not nouned [whispered].
> Herestow not the grete swogh?"
>   (II, 1025–1031)

Chaucer hears it; in fact the grete swogh puts him into a great
swete much as loud noises do human infants — not to mention what
infant swoghs do to human adults. But if sound quite divorced
from meaning is impressive — like thunder or the roar of surf,
Chaucer says — it is even more so when personalized, as the eagle
indicates:

> "But understond now ryght wel this:
> Whan any speche ycomen ys
> Up to the paleys, anon-ryght
> Hyt wexeth lyk the same wight
> Which that the word in erthe spak,
> Be hyt clothed red or blak,
> And hath so verray hys lyknesse
> That spak the word, that thou wilt gesse
> That it the same body be,
> Man or womman, he or she.
> And ys not this a wonder thyng?"
>   (II, 1073–1083)

The objective, sonant properties of speech that have produced

---

15 *House of Fame*, II, 765, in *The Poetical Works of Chaucer*, ed. F. N. Rob-
inson (Cambridge, Mass., 1933).

the frighteningly grete swogh, the surge of meaningless masses of air, materialize into human form. The house of Fame is certainly not the place where we would expect an ideal fusion of meaning and substance in speech, but Chaucer is surely playing with such a notion (just as he is playing more broadly with the problem of implanting some of the experiential stuff of life in the abstractly learned passenger-Chaucer). The corporealization of the word, at any rate, the creation of meaning not by means of but *in* language — so that sounds mean and meanings sound — this is the distinctly personal quality of all poetry worthy of the word. And ys not this a wonder thyng?

The point finally is that the poet does not stop with sound as masses of air in motion any more than sculptors stop with blocks of granite. The poet does his carving in sound. He is not content for instance with meter, which in itself reduces poetry toward mechanical regularity of a sort that Father Ong would rightfully object to, but by carving in sound he creates rhythm, which one might call humanized meter. It is this distinction that critics have made who have stressed literature's objective properties; they have not likened literature to blocks of stone or to canvas and oils but rather to statues, urns, ikons, and patterns — to objects that have been rendered aesthetic, particular, and distinctively individual.

IV

Romeo and Juliet

A FORMAL DWELLING

AS AN indirect entry to *Romeo and Juliet* let me dwell for a moment on Shakespeare's management of vows, since vows are especially good indices of a dramatist's conception of language in addition to having a strong bearing on character, motive, even dramatic form. In *Titus Andronicus* Shakespeare saw in the vow a formal principle of Senecan revenge tragedy. Out of the chaos of his material the dramatist contrives a teleology in which the vow serves as a structural promise to be redeemed by a culminating act of vengeance. The strangest vow in that strange play, however, is not Titus's vow of vengeance but Lucius's vow of mercy (in 5.1), which results from Aaron's insistence that unless his child goes free he like his descendant Iago "never will speak word." Shakespeare makes much of this contract between Lucius and Aaron partly because it introduces an element of mercy into a drama whose zestful cruelty makes Antonin Artaud's pronouncements on that subject seem saccharine by comparison but partly too because like so many other bizarre encounters in the play it figures his dramatic problem of uniting words and actions. The contract involves the exchange of Lucius's "word" for Aaron's "plot," and that is precisely the kind of contract Shakespeare has himself been trying without success to negotiate in *Titus Andronicus*. By spinning out the im-

plications of Lucius's vow one might arrive at a fairly good notion
of the central dramatic problem of the play.

Vows are equally significant in *Love's Labour's Lost*. In vow-
ing themselves to the life of Academe the scholars rely on the autonomy of words, not as they function in society but as defined,
purified, and sworn to by themselves. So constituted, words will
suppress nature in the form of the scholars' own "affections" and
"the huge army of the world's desires" (primarily women). Since
a purely private verbal world is impossible, their fragile fortress of
words collapses before the assaulting army of the world's desires
marching in petticoats from France. The scholars then scatter a
second set of vows during their Muscovite wooing scene, each to
the wrong lady, the disastrous effect of which suggests that if
words may be overvalued through private hoarding they may also
be undervalued through promiscuous spending. Behind the surface
plight of laboring lovers hiding behind words and then distributing
them wildly in all directions stands the poet's metadramatic plight
as he tries to arbitrate between the individual and private needs of
his art on the one hand and the all-too-public and debased nature of
the language in which his art must be cast. No solution to that
problem is arrived at in *Love's Labour's Lost*. Neither by trying to
virginize the universal whore language nor by trailing her about
the streets and risking contamination himself can the playwright
achieve the elusive and mysterious marriage of language and art
that will make him whole.

It is generally supposed that *Titus Andronicus* preceded
Love's Labour's Lost, and if so then the comedy may be seen as a
reaction to the would-be tragedy, a recoiling from violent action,
contrived plots, and stage sensationalism. The result is a purely verbal, plotless, essentially nondramatic work. Since it is also generally
supposed that *Love's Labour's Lost* preceded *Romeo and Juliet*
perhaps the latter can be considered in some degree at least as a response to the issues dealt with in the comic play. The marriage of
the hero and heroine for instance would seem to acquire special
significance in view of the conspicuous non-marriage of the lovers
in the earlier play. In *Love's Labour's Lost* marriage was conceived

of as the proper terminus of dramatic form, where the play ought to but perversely refuses to end, and as the product of a true language. Neither form nor language is discovered, however, and we are left with a mannered, courtly play of words illustrating its author's astonishing virtuosity but also, as he himself underscores by thrusting Mercade into the nonaction, a certain glib and glittering superficiality. The truth of the feelings is first suppressed by words and later distorted and obscured by them. As the purgative punishments of the scholars imply, the poet's language must somehow incorporate inner truth and outer reality, the mystery of love and such bleak facts of nature as time, suffering, death.

II

These then are the major metadramatic issues, at least on the side of language, confronting Shakespeare as he turns to *Romeo and Juliet*. From the problem of language he moves on in this play to the problem of dramatic form. But first let us focus on language and particularly on the balcony scene of 2.2 where vows again come into prominence. The place to begin is of course Juliet's famous complaint against the tyranny of names:

> 'Tis but thy name that is my enemy;
> Thou art thyself though not a Montague.
> What's Montague? It is nor hand nor foot
> Nor arm nor face nor any other part
> Belonging to a man. O be some other name!
> What's in a name? That which we call a rose
> By any other word would smell as sweet.
> So Romeo would, were he not Romeo called,
> Retain that dear perfection which he owes
> Without that title. Romeo, doff thy name,
> And for thy name, which is no part of thee,
> Take all myself.   (2.2.38-49)

Here and more widely throughout the play, brilliantly figured in the implicit metaphor of family and relatives, verbal nominalism is equated with a kind of social personalism. That is, in her anxiety to circumvent the opposition of their relatives Juliet would reject all relations and find ultimate truth in the haecceity, thisness, or as she puts it "dear perfection" of a totally unaffiliated Romeo. In the same way nominalism rejects the family or tribal relations of words in their more universal and abstract forms and situates verbal truth in the concrete and particular terms that seem most closely tied to the unique, unrelated, and hence true objects of which reality is composed. Juliet's nominalism here is a position with which the poet can readily sympathize,[1] because words come to the poet as Romeo comes to Juliet, trailing dark clouds of a prior public identity. Romeo comes to Juliet not merely from the streets of Verona and the house of Montague but from the shallows of Petrarchan love dotage as well, since he begins this play as Berowne ended his, an unrequited wooer of "Rosaline" (who is appropriately no more than a "name" in *Romeo and Juliet*). Juliet's verbal program is roughly analogous to that of the scholars of Navarre when they sought to establish their Academe. Where they tried to seal them-

[1] It is a position with which we can all sympathize, for that matter, since it reflects a recurrent human urge to scour our modes of apprehending experience, to brighten up a world that has been sicklied over by the pale cast of thought and drab expression. Anxious to purify Romeo of his family connections and meet him in all his shining individuality, Juliet might well approve of Husserl's desire for philosophy to return to things themselves, to let phenomena speak for themselves without the mediating and therefore presumably falsifying intervention of the mind with all its presuppositions (of which genus, or family, is surely a major meddler). However, the Hopkinsean "inscape" of man — the unique Romeo freed of his Montague associations — was less attractive to Renaissance moral philosophers, usually registered Platonists, who distinguished between two aspects of human nature — general and specific, genus and differentia — and felt that although the differentia made men interesting it was the genus that kept them civilized (see for instance Cicero's *Offices*, chapters 30 and 31). Juliet might want Romeo to be able to say "I am myself alone," but the man who actually says it is Richard Crookback at a major moment in a long and uniquely inhuman career (*3 Henry VI*, 5.6.83). In "The King's Language: Shakespeare's Drama as Social Discovery," *Antioch Review*, 21(1961):369–387, Sigurd Burckhardt has some brief but shrewd remarks about Juliet's nominalism; and for an excellent equation of nominalism and personalism see Murray Krieger's "The Existential Basis of Contextual Criticism" in *The Play and Place of Criticism* (Baltimore, 1967), pp. 239–251. In his interesting article "The Rose and Its Name: On Denomination in *Othello, Romeo and Juliet, Julius Caesar*," *Texas Studies in Literature and Language*, 11(1969):671–686, Manfred Weidhorn discusses the bondage of verbal categories from which the lovers are liberated by virtue of their meeting without introductions.

selves off from the outside world by founding an elite society on a private language, Juliet seeks to go even further, to rename or even "de-name" in the interests of purifying a Romeo who has been abroad with his pseudo-love.[2] (Of course Juliet does not know about Rosaline, but Shakespeare does, and thus has Juliet repudiate Petrarchan "form," "strangeness," and "cunning" a bit further on.)

Romeo is more than willing to be renamed —

> Call me but love and I'll be new baptized;
> Henceforth I never will be Romeo
>
> $(2.2.50-51)$

— but his language throughout the scene betrays him. Like Berowne, who prematurely thought himself cured of the Petrarchan style, Romeo still has "a trick/ Of the old rage" (*Love's Labour's Lost*, 5.2.416–417). It reveals itself most obviously when he begins keening vows:

> Lady, by yonder blessed moon I vow
> That tips with silver all these fruit-tree tops —
> JULIET. O swear not by the moon, the inconstant moon
> That monthly changes in her circled orb,
> Lest that thy love prove likewise variable.
> ROMEO. What shall I swear by?
> JULIET.   Do not swear at all.
> Or, if thou wilt, swear by thy gracious self,
> Which is the god of my idolatry,
> And I'll believe thee.
> ROMEO.   If my heart's dear love —
> JULIET. Well, do not swear. Although I joy in thee,
> I have no joy of this contract tonight.
> It is too rash, too unadvised, too sudden,
> Too like the lightning, which doth cease to be
> Ere one can say it lightens. Sweet, goodnight.
> This bud of love, by summer's ripening breath,
> May prove a beauteous flower when next we meet.
> Goodnight, goodnight! As sweet repose and rest

---

2 The walled orchard that isolates the lovers from the harsh realities of Veronese life is very much akin to the park of the scholars in *Love's Labour's Lost*, which was so rigorously declared off limits to foreign speech and female bodies.

Come to thy heart as that within my breast.
ROMEO. O wilt thou leave me so unsatisfied?
JULIET. What satisfaction canst thou have tonight?
ROMEO. The exchange of thy love's faithful vow for mine.

(2.2.107–127)

Like the scholars of Navarre in their wooing phase ("O who can give an oath?") Romeo is a ready spender of words and, also like them, naively trustful that vows can trace around lovers a magic circle to hold the devilish world at bay. But like the French ladies Juliet has a maturer conception of the laws of verbal contract and the power of their magic. Her rejection of the "inconstant moon" as a third party to the contract and her apprehensions about the rash, unadvised, and oversudden enlarge the more immediate threat of the feuding families to include all that is dangerously unstable beyond the periphery of private feeling. But she is also unsure of Romeo's love, which is available to her only as it is given shape in his language. Instinctively she distrusts his *style*, as Shakespeare forces us to notice by having her twice interrupt him as he cranks up his rhetorical engines in preparation for Petrarchan flights. Throughout this scene, and the play for that matter, it is Romeo's speech that soars airily and often vacuously. Juliet's, though hardly leaden, is more earthbound. She is not opposed to vows entirely — though her nominalism inevitably tends in that direction — but seeks a true language in which they may be expressed. Thus when Romeo selects the moon as a symbol of purity to swear by, she, recognizing the pseudo-purity of his own Petrarchan style, reminds him that the moon is also a symbol of inconstancy. Not the purling phrases rising easily to the lips of a thousand dandies with well-hinged knees but the genuine custom-made article is what she seeks:

> O gentle Romeo,
> If thou dost love, pronounce it faithfully.
> Or if thou think'st I am too quickly won
> I'll frown and be perverse and say thee nay —
> So thou wilt woo; but else, not for the world.
> In truth, fair Montague, I am too fond,

And therefore thou mayst think my 'haviour light.
But trust me, gentleman, I'll prove more true
Than those that have more cunning to be strange.

                                    (2.2.93–101)

"Pronounce it faithfully" — unfortunately Romeo, who would
forge a binding verbal contract, is himself bound to the book of
form. Like Paris, whom Lady Capulet lengthily describes as a "fair
volume" (1.3.79ff), and Tybalt, whom Mercutio despises as an
"antic, lisping, affecting fantastico" who stands "much on the new
form" (2.4.29–37) and "fights by the book of arithmetic" (3.1.105),
Romeo not only kisses "by the book" (1.5.112) but trumpets vows
by the book of Petrarchan form. Juliet admits that she *could* play
at Petrarchanism and that to do so might even invest her behavior
with an appearance of mature reserve that her forthrightness of
feeling makes her seem without. But even if a bit fondly, she specializes in truth, not form, and so concludes "but farewell compli-
ment!/Dost thou love me?" (2.2.89–90). Truly virginal, she recoils from the potential contamination of vows loosely and gran-
diloquently untethered: "Well, do not swear." Do not swear, do
not even speak — that is the end of the nominalistic line because
even at their best words cannot perfectly reflect the autonomous
individuality of objects, or in this case of genuine love. Seeking an
ideal communion of love at a level beyond idle breath, Juliet would
purify words quite out of existence and reduce dialogue to an exchange of intuition and sheer feeling — a marriage of true minds accomplished without the connective medium of language.

III

If we set Juliet's remarks on names in a literary perspective instead of a general nominalistic one they might be taken to suggest
an extreme toward which the lyric impulse sometimes tends, that is
an ineffable purity. Here it is an ineffable purity of love, but its
counterparts elsewhere would include the "unexpressive nuptial
song" mentioned by Milton in "Lycidas," that etherealized music in
Keats's "Ode on a Grecian Urn" —

> Heard melodies are sweet, but those unheard
> Are sweeter; therefore, ye soft pipes, play on;
> Not to the sensual ear, but, more endeared,
> Pipe to the spirit ditties of no tone

— and the dumb eloquence of lips in Hopkins's "The Habit of Perfection":

> Shape nothing, lips; be lovely-dumb:
> It is the shut, the curfew sent
> From there where all surrenders come
> Which only makes you eloquent.

Such scattered examples remind us of how its recurrent attraction to the pure and ideal leads lyric toward seclusion from the ruck and reel of time, action, and the world. Etymologically, though not always in practice, lyric aspires to the condition of music, seeking to purify noise into melody and sometimes even, as expressed in the examples above, to a point beyond sound, to stillness. Similarly as regards time and motion, lyric would discover a terminal rest, a retreat from the hurly-burly of action and consequences where thought and feeling crystallize in an expressive stasis. Murray Krieger has demonstrated the apt ambiguity of the word "still" to express in terms of motion the ever-moving fixity of poetry as it sets progressive experience within a transfixing form or, in Yeatsian language, unites the dancer with the dance.[3] In talking about *Romeo and Juliet*, however, we need to enlarge on the ambiguities of stillness by adding silence to the ever-neverness of motion since Juliet, as we have seen, would reduce love's dialogue to a silent communion of unique, inexpressible feeling.

Shakespeare, it is time to say, is abundantly aware how foolish such a *reductio ad silentium* must be from the standpoint of the poet. However intense his own longing to attain a purity out of the swing of speech — and it seems to me considerably so — he knows with Mallarmé that poetry is written with words, not ideas, and especially not ideas before which the poet must become breathless with adoration. If Juliet's view were to prevail the play would turn

---

3   See "The Ekphrastic Principle and the Still Movement of Poetry; or *Laokoön* Revisited" in *The Play and Place of Criticism*, pp. 105–128.

mute and time stand still, or at least slow down to the point where nine o'clock tomorrow takes twenty years to arrive (2.2.168–170). Drama would dissolve into lyric and lyric would dissolve into a silent center of inexpressible love surrounded by the cacophony of the street scenes, the nurse's babble and Mercutio's bawdry, the expostulations of Capulet, and the intoned sententia of Friar Laurence.

The plight of the poet who would retreat within lyric to a purer wordlessness is humorously illustrated when Juliet, after appropriately hearing "some noise within" and retiring briefly to investigate, returns to the balcony and cannot momentarily locate Romeo:

> JULIET. Hist! Romeo, hist! O for a falconer's voice
> To lure this tassel-gentle back again!
> Bondage is hoarse, and may not speak aloud,
> Else would I tear the cave where Echo lies
> And make her airy tongue more hoarse than mine
> With repetition of my Romeo's name.
> Romeo!   (2.2.159–165)

If "Necessity" as Berowne said could make the scholars "all forsworn/ Three thousand times within this three years' space" (*Love's Labour's Lost*, 1.1.150–151), it can also make a sorely frustrated Juliet acknowledge the indispensability of names within a little more than a hundred lines of her great protest against them. In that brief space the tyrannous "bondage" of verbal categories (locking the free spirit of reality into claustrophobic linguistic cells) metamorphoses into its opposite, the "bondage" that prevents Juliet from giving full free voice to that most useful category "Romeo." For the lovers and for the poet Shakespeare the notion of establishing communion on a plane of feeling transcending the imperfections of speech is "but a dream/ Too flattering-sweet to be substantial" (2.2.140–141). Not only must the lovers rely on names for the rudiments of communication, but their love itself becomes a great name-singing celebration:

> ROMEO. It is my soul that calls upon my name.
> How silver-sweet sound lovers' tongues by night,

Like softest music to attending ears!

(2.2.165–167)

JULIET.   . . . and every tongue that speaks
But Romeo's name speaks heavenly eloquence.

(3.2.32–33)

That Juliet somewhat humorously belies herself in this last quotation, finding a "heavenly eloquence" in the name she earlier thought inimical to their love, is in keeping with a play that seems founded on the principle of the oxymoron: she wants, it seems, a "nameless naming." The paradox metadramatically reflects the difficulty of Shakespeare's own situation as he wrestles in this play with the slipperiest of antagonists, verbal purity, against whom even he may be overmatched. It is a contest waged between every poet and language, and it ends for better or worse in a compromise somewhere between the private dream and the public fact. The contest is the more arduous for being conducted within the ring of drama where the impulse to verbal purity takes the form of lyric, which retards, as opposed to action, which impels. I'll get back to this particular issue later; for the moment I need to isolate the linguistic problem from the more embracing dramatic one.

If one charted the private/public range of language in *Romeo and Juliet*, at the furthest private extreme would come "silence," a nominalistic tendency so rigorous as to still speech entirely. Obviously since we do have a script for the play this extreme does not become manifest, except at those moments during performances when the lovers exchange prolonged glances and wordless sighs. Still at this end of the chart would appear the lovers' language within the orchard — self-cherishing, insular, answerable only to private feeling. At the extreme public end of the chart opposite silence is noise, disturbance, disquiet — the "airy word" of the opening scene which the Prince says has "thrice disturbed the quiet of our streets" with civil brawls. (The Prince is significantly more concerned with "peace" as quiet than as cessation of hostilities; the greatest threat to the play is sheer noise, its consistent goal harmonic sound.) Also at this end of the scale despite its affectation of privacy and purity is Romeo's Petrarchan language, full of sighs, show, and manner, and far too "airy" in its own way, as Juliet instantly perceives, to substantialize love in any genuine form. Here too, though antagonistic to Romeo's Petrarchanism, is Mercutio's ribald wordplay, as amusingly impure verbally as the sensuality it dotes on is in comparison to Romeo and Juliet's love.

One would also expect to place Friar Laurence's "holy words" within the public sphere since it is through the public institutions of church and marriage, by having "Holy Church incorporate two in one," that the friar hopes to reunite the oppugnant families. That would seem an ideal union, the private bond of love becoming a public bond of marriage sealing the families, because although love itself may be a fine and private thing marriage is by nature public. Its function is to translate private feeling into the received language of society and so give public residence to what may otherwise be simply emotional vagrancy — unpropertied, subjective, and strange. This love, we know, transcends all that. But nonetheless the wedding *is* private, and the marriage it begets remains so. Consecrated by holy words, the lovers' vows bind them to one another (suggesting that the language of love's communion so absent from *Love's Labour's Lost* has been discovered) but in this private union they remain divorced from the wider social context into which genuine marriage would incorporate them.

Their love then is translated into a language that goes unheard beyond the narrow circle formed by themselves, the friar, and later the nurse. Alone in the privacy of his cell Friar Laurence can celebrate the sacrament of Communion, can give quiet voice to *the* Word (Logos), and have its spiritual benefits circulate among all men. But he cannot do so with the sacrament of marriage. If marriage is to be the medium of a secular, familial communion, its sacramental language must be heard by the fallen families it would save, and in that regard the friar's words are as inaudible as those of the lovers. The most obvious symbol of the friar's inability to give public circulation to his own and the lovers' language is his short-circuited letter to Romeo in Mantua. Like Romeo when he leaves the orchard haven for the brawling streets, the friar's words — sur-

rogates for the lovers' words — run afoul of the "infectious pesti-
lence" of the outside world (5.2.10). (Mercutio's curse "A plague
o' both your houses" is thus most literally fulfilled by the plague
that detains Friar John.) Despite his intentions then Friar Laurence
is less a mediator between private and public spheres than a religious
version of the private — his rather monastic celibacy suggesting an
analogue to the withdrawn lyric adoration of the lovers. Only
when the lovers are dead and he Horatio-like tells their story does
the friar finally marry them to the social order and bind the families as he had hoped.

Through neither family nor church can love make its way into
the social context, nor through a third major institution, the state.
As a political entity the Veronese state is elusive to the vanishing
point; its dramatic form is simply the voice of the Prince, quite literally his sentences. In the opening scene ("hear the sentence of
your moved prince") he decrees death to anyone who breaks the
peace, and in 3.1 he pronounces sentence on Romeo ("A gentler
judgment vanished from his lips," the friar reports, "Not body's
death but body's banishment" — 3.3.10–11). From one standpoint
the princely word is not good since the peace it ordained is subse-
quently broken and the banished body returns; from another it is,
since Mercutio and Tybalt die for their offense and Romeo for his
(the Prince had said "when [Romeo's] found that hour is his last,"
and so it is — 3.1.200). The political word clearly has its limits — as
when the citizen, unaware that Tybalt is dead, cries "Up, sir, go
with me. / I charge thee in the Prince's name, obey" (3.1.144–145) [4]
— but it also has its sovereignty, as Juliet laments:

> "Romeo is banished!" To speak that word
> Is father, mother, Tybalt, Romeo, Juliet,
> All slain, all dead. "Romeo is banished!"
> There is no end, no limit, measure, bound,
> In that word's death; no words can that woe sound.
>
> (3.2.122–126)

4 In performances of the play it is sometimes assumed that the citizen addresses a kneeling Benvolio rather than a dead Tybalt. But Benvolio has just
said "There lies that Tybalt," not "here" as he would if he were kneeling over
him. The citizen, greatly concerned to take Tybalt in, is inattentive to mat-

If the Prince's word cannot spring the dead to life and duty as the citizen demanded, it can afflict the living with death.

The major emphasis in 3.2 and 3.3, in which the word "banished" is repeated nineteen times, is to force on the lovers the anti-nominalist realization that although as Juliet said a name is "nor hand nor foot/ Nor arm nor face nor any other part/ Belonging to a man," even so airily universal a verb as "banished" can permanently still all those moving parts:

> JULIET. That "banished," that one word "banished,"
> Hath slain ten thousand Tybalts.
>
> (3.2.113–114)

> JULIET.   To speak that word
> Is father, mother, Tybalt, Romeo, Juliet,
> All slain, all dead.   (3.2.122–124)

> ROMEO.   Calling death "banishment"
> Thou cut'st my head off with a golden axe.
>
> (3.3.21–22)

If the language of love is inaudible to society, the language of society is deafening to the lovers. From such clangor the only final escape is to the quiet of the grave.

IV

"Banished" is the severing word that immediately threatens and finally destroys the communion of love since because of it the lovers are forced to communicate through society by means of the friar's message, and that is precisely what they cannot do. Only in a state of lyric seclusion hermetically sealed off from the plague-stricken world outside can their language retain its expressive purity. But the lovers cannot remain forever in the orchard, much as they would like to, and the poet cannot escape the fact that whereas his art is private, wrought in his own stylistic image and even given that personal signature that Shakespeare laments in Sonnet 76, his linguistic medium itself is intransigently public. As part of

ters such as death, Hamlet's "fell sergeant" who is more "strict in his arrest" even than vigilante citizens.

the vulgar tongue the words he would adopt are contaminated by ill usage, by an ever-present epidemic of imprecision, banality, lies, false rhetoric, jargon, true rhetoric, sentimentality, and solecisms, and by more localized historical plagues such as Petrarchanism, Euphuism, inkhorn neologisms, television commercials, social scientese, and beat or hippie nonspeak. Like Juliet on first confronting Romeo, the poet wants to compel words to abandon their corrupt public identities and submit to his cleansing rebaptism. Or again, to use another of the play's metaphors, like Romeo words as public identities must die ("He heareth not, he stirreth not, he moveth not" Mercutio says of Romeo; "The ape is dead" — 2.1.15–16) so that they may be reborn within the context of the poem ("Call me but love and I'll be new baptized;/ Henceforth I never will be Romeo" — 2.2.50–51).

This account of things is perhaps unduly metaphoric and a bit confusing as regards Romeo, whose verbal status is rather ambiguous. His Petrarchan style is impure, as underscored by Juliet's stylistic objections, because in the context of the play it comes from that extramural world outside the orchard. That is not to say that the sonnets of Wyatt, Sidney, Spenser, or Petrarch himself exhibit corrupt language. It is to say that the Petrarchan *style* has a public existence outside individual Petrarchan poems and that in Shakespeare's time — and certainly in his own view, as Sonnet 130 makes clear — it stood for a debased literary currency. Paradoxically at least some of this impurity derives from the fact that the Petrarchan style aspires to pure poetry and in so aspiring becomes an airy, hyperbolic, mechanically artificial expression of unfelt and undiscriminating feelings. In this sense it is too pure ("Virtue itself turns vice, being misapplied" — 2.3.21), and when the too pure becomes too popular it turns impure, an infectious blight on the literary landscape.

From this excessive purity excessively available, Juliet recoils, seeking like Shakespeare a more individual style, a more genuine purity. But neither Juliet nor Shakespeare fully succeeds in the attempt to forge a new and authentic idiom. We are clearly asked to regard the movement from Romeo-Rosaline to Romeo-Juliet as an

advance from Petrarchan dotage to true romantic love. And surely
in large degree it is — after all, this love seals its bond in marriage
and bears it out even to and beyond the edge of doom. Granted,
and yet I doubt that either we or Shakespeare can rest fully at ease
with the lovers' style. The trouble is that the old Romeo is imper-
fectly killed off; the ape is not really dead — too much of his Petrarchan manner and language live on in him; and Juliet, despite her
anti-Petrarchan bias, too readily quickens to the invitations of his
style. Her better speeches are resistance pieces that gain eloquence
in the process of denying the power of speech itself, most notably
in the balcony scene. She scores well off Romeo's verbal extravagance:

> ROMEO. Ah Juliet, if the measure of thy joy
> Be heaped like mine, and that thy skill be more
> To blazon it, then sweeten with thy breath
> This neighbour air and let rich music's tongue
> Unfold the imagined happiness that both
> Receive in either by this dear encounter.
> JULIET. Conceit, more rich in matter than in words,
> Brags of his substance, not of ornament.
> They are but beggars that can count their worth,
> But my true love is grown to such excess
> I cannot sum up sum of half my wealth.
>
> (2.6.25–34)

But if the worth of private feeling cannot be assessed in the crude
countinghouse of language, Juliet seems not always aware of it.
This is most noticeable when on learning that Romeo has killed
Tybalt her feelings swing from love to dismay:

> O serpent heart hid with a flowering face!
> Did ever dragon keep so fair a cave?
> Beautiful tyrant! Fiend angelical!
> Dove-feathered raven! Wolvish ravening lamb!
> Despised substance of divinest show!
>
> (3.2.73–77)

The distinction in the last line between substance and show invites our recollection of the distinction between substance and ornament in her speech just quoted (2.6.30–31) and urges on us the

stylistic reversal that has occurred. It is wonderfully fitting that Juliet should register the shock to private feeling by adopting Romeo's Petrarchan oxymorons (cf. 1.1.181–188) at the exact moment when her loyalties turn in the antinominalist direction of "family" (she grieves not for Tybalt the unique but for Tybalt the cousin). She quickly recovers from this style and feeling, as does their love in general, but in the remainder of the scene her style (like Romeo's in 3.3) keeps shrilling upward into a mannered hysteria in which conceit, less rich in matter than in words, brags of its ornament, not its substance. Bathos is now their medium, and their verbal excesses are defended on the authority of unique feeling:

> ROMEO. Thou canst not speak of that thou dost not feel.
> Wert thou as young as I, Juliet thy love,
> An hour but married, Tybalt murdered,
> Doting like me and like me banished,
> Then mightst thou speak, then mightst thou tear thy hair
> And fall upon the ground as I do now,
> Taking the measure of an unmade grave.   (3.3.64–70)

Such claims disarm criticism — ours I suppose as well as that of the friar, who must be wincing at the amount of hypothesis required to put him in the position of youth and love. No one denies the validity and intensity of the feeling, but of course a riot of feeling need not necessitate a riot of language and premature measurements of graves that look suspiciously like cribs. Romeo rejects all discipline that originates beyond self, whether moral, social, or stylistic. In effect he repudiates the world, and so hastens logically on to the notion of suicide. When Friar Laurence, harried back and forth across the room by the banging of the world at his door and the blubbering of a Romeo who would dissolve all connections with the world, cries in exasperation "What simpleness is this!" (3.3.77) his choice of the noun is perfect, for in the unblended simpleness of Romeo the man of unique feelings there is indeed at this point great silliness. However, Romeo is not altogether as pure in his simpleness as he would like, and radical purgation is called for:

> O tell me, friar, tell me
> In what vile part of this anatomy
> Doth my name lodge? Tell me, that I may sack
> The hateful mansion.
>
> (3.3.105–108)

To become pure "Romeo" and extirpate his connections with everything beyond self he would destroy "Montague," the "vile part" of him in which the world has staked its claim. But as the friar points out, the dagger that pierces Montague pierces Romeo as well:

> Why rail'st thou on thy birth, the heaven, and earth?
> Since birth and heaven and earth all three do meet
> In thee at once, which thou at once wouldst lose.
>
> (3.3.119–121)

So far as I can see there is small evidence that Romeo absorbs much of the friar's lesson. For him there remains no world beyond the walls of Juliet's garden, where the lovers still strive to meet with all the nominalistic singularity of their Edenic forebears. Their lamentations in 3.2 and 3.3 are only a more strident stylistic version of their speech in 3.5. In this the last scene in which they engage in genuine dialogue before the destructive force of the word "banished" takes its full toll, we see the lyric imagination desperately seeking to impose its own truth on the world of fact and sunrise:

> JULIET. Wilt thou be gone? It is not yet near day.
> It was the nightingale and not the lark
> That pierced the fearful hollow of thine ear.
> Nightly she sings on yond pomegranate tree.
> Believe me, love, it was the nightingale.
>
> (3.5.1–5)

And again:

> JULIET. Yond light is not daylight, I know it, I —
> It is some meteor that the sun exhales
> To be to thee this night a torchbearer
> And light thee on thy way to Mantua.
>
> (3.5.12–15)

In line with her nominalistic "A rose by any other word" Juliet would rebaptize Nature, transforming lark and daylight into night-ingale and meteor to the end that time stand still. Romeo allows himself to be persuaded that "it is not day," but as soon as he does so Juliet's lyric preoccupation is gone: "It is, it is! Hie hence, be gone, away!" (3.5.25–26). As it operates in the wide world, language may be less pure than the lovers would wish, but it stands for a view of reality that neither lover nor poet can safely ignore. Time, light, larks, and the usual terms for them remain intransi-gently themselves, answerable to their public definitions. The lover who withdraws entirely from the world into an autistic domain of feeling must pay for his pleasure with his life, as Romeo would were he to remain in the orchard. By the same token the poet who reshapes language in the exclusive light of his own designs, turning his back on his audience and creating not a truly individual but merely a unique style, must pay for his eccentric pleasures with his poetic life. There is no great danger of that here since the trouble with the lovers' style is not eccentricity but conventionality. The purity it aspires to, like that of the Petrarchanism to which it is un-comfortably akin, is too easily come by. And judging their lan-guage this way, I should be quick to add — that is, grading it down for poetic diction and a superabundance of rhetorical figures — is not to impose on the play a modern bias against rhetoric but to ac-cept the implications of the play itself and to honor Shakespeare's own standards, which are implicit in his gradual estrangement over the years from an enameled, repetitive, lyrical style in favor of one that is concentrated, complex, and dramatic.

V

It would seem then that in *Romeo and Juliet* Shakespeare has encountered but by no means resolved the poet's dilemma. No doubt he must often have known perfectly well where he wanted poetically to go and yet could not get there, and knew that too. On the authority of the play's structure we can assume that he wanted to get from Rosaline to Juliet, from pure poetry to a viable poetic purity, but that he did not complete the journey in satisfactory style. That he realized this seems evident from the care he has taken to protectively enclose the lovers' poetic purity. Robert Penn Warren has shrewdly argued that the "impure poetry" of Mercutio and the nurse — poetry, that is, that reflects the impurity of life itself by means of wit, irony, logical contradictions, jagged rhythms, unpoetic diction, and so forth — provides a stylistic context in which we can more readily accept the too pure poetry of the lovers.[5] Warren assumes in other words that the impure poetry in the play functions much as William Empson claims comic subplots function, as lightning rods to divert the audience's potentially dyslogistic reactions away from the vulnerable high seriousness of the main plot (main style).[6] The implication is that Shakespeare is trying to have it both ways at once, that like Juliet asking for an "unnamed naming" in the balcony scene he asks us to accept the authenticity of a style that he himself knows is too pure and therefore needful of protection. From this perspective one sees that in stacking the literary deck against the lovers — by providing the stylistic opposition of Mercutio and the nurse and the environmental opposition of the feuding families, of fate, coincidences, and mistimings — Shakespeare has actually stacked it in their favor. The obvious contrast is with *Antony and Cleopatra*, and we might note that whereas the impure poetry of Enobarbus functions like that of Mercutio and the nurse, by that time Shakespeare has mastered his own stylistic problems and can imbue those lovers' language with an impurity of its own. If the later technique risks more, it stands to gain more too, and as we all know does.

The argument made here in terms of style can be extended to character and genre also, for the lovers themselves, no less than their style, are too pure and they acquire in the minds of too many readers an unearned tragic stature. Even though the play rejects uniqueness Shakespeare has nominalistically bleached from Romeo and Juliet most of the impurities that rub off on man by virtue of

5 In his famous article "Pure and Impure Poetry" originally printed in the *Kenyon Review*, 5 (Spring 1943):228–254, and since reprinted in many collections of critical essays.

6 Empson's remarks on subplots appear in *Some Versions of Pastoral*, pp. 25–84 of the New Directions paperback edition (New York, 1960).

his public contacts. They simply have no public contacts. Despite the importance of family, they are essentially unrelated, meeting as isolated individuals rather than (like Antony and Cleopatra) as complex human beings with social, political, religious, and even national allegiances and responsibilities to contend with. Insufficiently endowed with complexity, with the self-division that complexity makes possible, and with the self-perceptiveness that such division makes possible, they become a study in victimage and sacrifice, not tragedy. Their experience portrays not the erosion within but the clash without, and the plot harries them toward lamentation instead of vision. One of the major ironies of the final scene in the tomb is that for all its imagery of radiance the illumination is entirely outside Romeo, kindled by torches and Juliet's beauty, not by a self-reflective consciousness. On the stylistic failure as it relates to tragedy Maynard Mack says "Comic overstatement aims at being preposterous. Until it becomes so, it remains flat. Tragic overstatement, on the other hand, aspires to be believed, and unless in some sense it is so, remains bombast."[7]

In Shakespeare's protection of the lovers Mercutio plays a crucial role, for although Juliet rejects the false purity of Romeo's Petrarchan style she never has to encounter the rich impurity of Mercutio's speech. And it is Mercutio who seems the genuine threat. The nurse's style is abundantly impure, but that is all it is, whereas Mercutio can deliver pure poetry impurely. In his much-admired, much-maligned Queen Mab speech, which looks so suspiciously and conspicuously irrelevant to the main issues of the play, Mercutio turns pure poetry back on itself. Even while presenting a lengthy illustration of pure poetry he defines it as a product of fancy and foolishness airily roaming like Queen Mab herself through dreaming minds, to which it offers substitute gratifications that have no direct bearing on reality — on real courtier's real curtsies and suits, on lawyer's stunning fees, ladies' kisses, parsons' benefices, soldiers' battles. "Peace, Mercutio, peace!" Romeo cries.

7   Maynard Mack, "The Jacobean Shakespeare: Some Observations on the Construction of the Tragedies," in *Jacobean Theatre*, vol. 1 of Stratford-upon-Avon Studies, ed. John Russell Brown and Bernard Harris (New York, 1960), p. 15.

"Thou talk'st of nothing." But because Mercutio can talk of something as well as nothing, because he can deal in both pure and impure styles, he is given a tough and enduring eloquence that makes
the nurse, mired in the language of sensual expedience, seem gross
and Romeo callow. (Romeo to be sure can vie with Mercutio in the
lubricities of street speech, but Romeo-with-Juliet is another man
altogether; Shakespeare keeps the two scrupulously discrete.)

Entering the orchard where felt experience is sovereign, Romeo can dismiss Mercutio's extramural ribaldry about Rosaline
with a famous line — "He jests at scars that never felt a wound" (2.
2.1). When the wound is in the other chest though, Romeo must
play straight man to more famous lines:

> ROMEO. Courage, man, the hurt cannot be much.
> MERCUTIO. No, 'tis not so deep as a well nor so wide as a
> church door, but 'tis enough, 'twill serve.
>
> (3.1.98–100)

This asks to be compared to the lovers' style. They repeatedly
claim that language is too shallow a thing to reach into the deeps of
private feeling, but their own verbal practice is hardly consistent
with such a claim. Whenever their feelings are touched, torrents
follow. Hence the bristling oxymorons of the stricken Romeo in
1.1 —

> Why then O brawling love! O loving hate!
> O anything, of nothing first create!
> O heavy lightness, serious vanity,
> Misshapen chaos of well-seeming forms!
> Feather of lead, bright smoke, cold fire, sick health!
> Still-waking sleep that is not what it is!
> This love feel I, that feel no love in this.
>
> (1.1.182–188)

Hence the same oxymorons from Juliet's lips in 3.2 ("Beautiful ty-
rant! fiend angelical!" etc.) and the bathos of Romeo in 3.3, for example —

> Heaven is here
> Where Juliet lives, and every cat and dog
> And little mouse, every unworthy thing,

> Live here in heaven and may look on her,
> But Romeo may not.   (3.3.29–33)

It is in this context of grotesque verbal posturing, where convulsions of speech coalesce with tantrums of feeling, that Mercutio's words on death acquire a quiet and sustained eloquence. It is those words ironically that best fulfill the stylistic requirements of Juliet's early nominalism. The uniquely felt inner "hurt" Mercutio does not try directly to define, thus avoiding the risks of hyperbole and general verbal inflation that prey on the speech of the lovers when they reflect on *their* wounds. The private feeling that's past the size of speech is suggested only obliquely, in terms of the size of the physical "hurt," and even then by saying not what it is but what it is not. Here in the plain style is functional language, language that like the wound itself is content to be "enough," to "serve" rather than run riot. In general then it is the mixed tones of Mercutio's speech that the lovers most need to incorporate into their own style. But Shakespeare has kept Mercutio permanently stationed on the outer side of the orchard wall, as oblivious to the existence of their love as they are to him.

The public world is too crass and bellicose to assimilate the private truth of love, and Mercutio is a good instance of the fact that there are public truths that the lovers cannot assimilate. Given two such disjunctive languages, only mutual injury remains possible. The lovers' language fails when it seeks to make its way by means of Father John through the plague-ridden world beyond the orchard. Love's feelings hold constant, but during the reunion in the tomb the dialogue of love dissolves into lyric monologues heard only by the speaker. One further step remains. The purity of their love (figured after Romeo's departure in Juliet's resistance to marrying Paris) is reasserted in a second marriage ceremony that is even more private than the first:

> ROMEO. Arms, take your last embrace. And lips, O you
> The doors of breath, seal with a righteous kiss
> A dateless bargain to engrossing death!
> (5.3.113–115)

In this final contract the breath of lyric speech and the breath of life are simultaneously expended to seal an endless bond with silence. So too with Juliet, who retreats into a remoter stillness as the noise of the outside world rushes toward her:

> Yea, noise? Then I'll be brief. O happy dagger!
> This is thy sheath. There rest and let me die.
>
> (5.3.169–170)

As the *Liebestod* stressed by Denis de Rougemont and others, Romeo and Juliet's love has been a flight from the frustrations of life toward the consummations of the grave. Similarly, as *Liebestille* their linguistic style has been a flight from noise toward a silence beyond speech. The silence is at last achieved and with it an expressiveness that extends their own bond of feeling outward. For embraced in and by death their still figures bespeak the truth of their love to the wondering representatives of the social order gathered in the tomb, and do so with such persuasiveness that it transforms those random and rancorous individuals into a genuine community united in sorrow and sympathy. The cost, however, runs high. What is purchased is in the Prince's apt phrase a "glooming peace" — peace as public amity has been bought by the sacrifice of the lovers to the peace of an enduring but eloquent stillness.

VI

Neither in life nor through language then do the lovers make connections with their social order or the wide world beyond the orchard. Self-engrossed to the end, their speech admits no impediments, not even death. Death in fact is less an impediment than a goal, a terminal value whose stillness, privacy, and endlessness sum up the character of their love. In this final marriage to death they divorce the world.

It goes without saying that there is a sentimentality about the ending of the play that goes down hard — the bravura notes of Romeo's final speeches, the pathetic suicides, the stagy recognition scene that seems framed to fulfill the child's morbidly gratifying wish to be present at his own imagined funeral. But Shakespeare is

not merely pumping up the pathos in order to celebrate the abso-
luteness of a fine and constant love done in by a crass society; he is
also attempting to negotiate between private and public values. In
comedy such negotiations are fulfilled in weddings that incorporate private love into the larger social context. In tragedy the division between private and public values is normally bridged by
sacrifice: the hero's alienating uniqueness becomes through his sacrificial death the instrument that binds his survivors to one another
and to his now lost and lamented value. So it is with Romeo and
Juliet. Though divorced from the world, as "poor sacrifices" they
bring about the marriage of the divided society they leave behind.
With this wider social marriage the play finds its formal resolution,
and so it is ultimately to Shakespeare's maturing concept of dramatic form that the lovers are sacrificed.

Before turning to the question of dramatic form, though, let
me note briefly how the statues to be erected by the bereaved fa-
thers confirm the success of sacrifice in bringing about fulfillment
in both private and public spheres:

> MONTAGUE.   But I can give thee more.
> For I will raise her statue in pure gold,
> That whiles Verona by that name is known
> There shall no figure at such rate be set
> As that of true and faithful Juliet.
>   CAPULET. As rich shall Romeo's by his lady's lie,
> Poor sacrifices of our enmity.
>
> (5.3.298–304)

The statues become the final emblem of that expressive stillness to
which the lovers' language has been implicitly devoted since the
balcony scene. However, the nominalistic purity to which they
had aspired is now transcended since the private meaning and value
of their love, as given expression in the silent gold figures, will be
made permanently public.

The verbal recoil of the play from noise toward expressive
stillness is the more apparent if we analyze the play in terms of an
economic or commercial motif that also culminates in the statues.
Briefly, the lovers' self-valuation stresses pricelessness, the impos-

sibility of "selling" their love to the two families or the public —
especially to Juliet's father, who feudalistically regards marriage as
a business transaction. To Romeo Juliet is a "jewel" precious beyond price (the nurse at one point, incidentally, calls her "Jule"):
"Beauty too rich for use, for earth too dear" (1.5.48–49). To Capulet she is "the hopeful lady of my earth" (1.2.15) — his *fille de terre*,
or "heiress" — who, however, because she is an unmarketable commodity by virtue of prior commitment to Romeo will finally in-
herit only enough of his land to make a grave (5.3.297). And Juliet
says of herself:

> They are but beggars that can count their worth;
> But my true love is grown to such excess
> I cannot sum up sum of half my wealth.
>
> (2.6.32–34)

Paradoxically then Montague "will raise her statue in pure gold"
(5.3.299). The effect of doing so will be on the one hand to reduce
Juliet to the base metal of public commerce but on the other hand
to cast that metal in an unnegotiable form. As pure gold statuary
the lovers retain a pricelessness that transcends commercial distri-
bution even while their value is "sold" in the sense of its being publicly shared. This selling of a priceless commodity is an exact equivalent in commercial terms to the "expressive stillness" we spoke of
on the linguistic plane.

So much for the verbal-commercial aspects of the statues' nonverbal expressiveness — though their very nonverbalness is an issue
to which we will return in the next section. I have so far dealt with
the stillness of the statues as "silence," but to give the analysis a
turn toward dramatic form I need to stress the motionlessness of
stillness. The gold that was so much the object of commercial voyages in Shakespeare's time and that once discovered and minted
went its endless voyage from pocket to pocket finds in the shape of
the statues a permanent rest. So does Romeo, who says more than
he knows when he prepares for his suicide:

> O here
> Will I set up my everlasting rest

> And shake the yoke of inauspicious stars
> From this world-wearied flesh.
>
> $(5.3.109-112)$

Romeo's experience in the play is depicted among other things as a voyage.[8] Setting off for what will become his first meeting with Juliet he says

> But He that hath the steerage of my course
> Direct my sail! $(1.4.112-113)$

Again in the balcony scene:

> I am no pilot, yet wert thou as far
> As that vast shore washed with the farthest sea
> I should adventure for such merchandise.
>
> $(2.2.82-85)$

And finally after his "O here/ Will I set up my everlasting rest":

> Come, bitter conduct, come, unsavoury guide!
> Thou desperate pilot, now at once run on
> The dashing rocks thy sea-sick weary bark.
>
> $(5.3.116-118)$

Thus Romeo voyages through the play to the final port of everlasting rest, which is both the grave and the gold statue commissioned by Capulet. In the form of the statue he embodies the paradox of motionless movement, a dynamic illusion of life artistically arrested — always moving and never moving in the same sense that an "everlasting rest" is both intransitive and ceaseless, a restless rest.[9]

However, motion is more pervasive in the play than this. There is the violent motion or commotion, the street fighting, with which everything begins; there is the balcony scene contract that Juliet calls

---

8 Moody Prior was the first, I think, to point out the pattern of this voyaging imagery, in *The Language of Tragedy* (New York, 1947), pp. 69–70.

9 "Stillness" as figured in the statues thus takes on the oxymoronic everneverness of Keats's urn and the other instances of literary ekphrasis analyzed by Murray Krieger in "The Ekphrastic Principle and the Still Movement of Poetry; or *Laokoön* Revisited."

> too rash, too unadvised, too sudden,
> Too like the lightning which doth cease to be
> Ere one can say it lightens   (2.2.118–120)

and the quick clandestine wedding that Romeo ("O let us hence; I stand on sudden haste") forces against the friar's counsels of moderation ("Wisely and slow — they stumble that run fast" — 2.3.93–94). There are also Mercutio itching for action, and the pell-mell Tybalt anxious for a grave; the immediacy of Romeo's banishment by the Prince ("Let Romeo hence in haste,/ Else when he's found that hour is his last"); the relentless rush of time as the Thursday of Juliet's enforced marriage to Paris is tolled on by Capulet the perpetual-motion matchmaker —

> Day, night, hour, tide, time, work, play,
> Alone, in company, still my care hath been
> To have her matched;   (3.5.178–180)

the speed of Romeo's return from Mantua; and finally the death-dealing liveliness of the poisons ("O true apothecary!/ Thy drugs are quick" — 5.3.119–120).[10]

The world at large rushes and the lovers haste toward one another, but when they are united, especially within the orchard, time and motion cease. Given the contrasting principles of movement and stasis, the form of the play might be diagrammed as a horizontal line interrupted by several circles indicating the times (in 1.5, 2.2, 2.6, 3.5, and 5.3) when Romeo and Juliet are together. For in each of these five scenes the primary tension is between staying and departing, and in each scene the lovers are called out of stillness by the exigencies of time and motion. In 1.5 they have been stilled in a kiss ("Then move not while my prayer's effect I take" — 108) but are interrupted by the nurse calling Juliet to her mother. In 2.2 Romeo starts to leave but is called back by Juliet, who then forgets why she did so; their next lines play on stillness in time and space:

10   This generalized haste of time and action has been frequently noted, perhaps most significantly in Brents Stirling's chapter "They Stumble That Run Fast" in *Unity in Shakespearean Tragedy* (New York, 1956).

> ROMEO. Let me stand here till thou remember it.
> JULIET. I shall forget, to have thee still stand there,
> Remembering how I love thy company.
> ROMEO. And I'll still stay, to have thee still forget,
> Forgetting any other home but this.
>
> (2.2.172–176)

But at their backs they always hear the nurse's voice clucking Juliet in and Romeo away (2.2.136, 149, 151). In 2.6 they are so transfixed by one another that the friar must pun heavily on leaving and staying even to get them to their own wedding:

> Come, come with me, and we will make short work,
> For, by your leaves, you shall not stay alone
> Till Holy Church incorporate two in one.
>
> (2.6.35–37)

And in 3.5 a world of clocks and irreversible sunrises tolls for Romeo, who "must be gone and live or stay and die" (11).

Staying a moment ourselves, we should observe that Shakespeare has here reversed the situation in *Love's Labour's Lost* in which the faint linear thrust of dramatic action was constantly diverted and absorbed into the circular eddies of lyric. If one of the things Shakespeare learned in that play is the inability of lyric speech to substitute for dramatic action, the effects of that lesson on *Romeo and Juliet* are apparent in the way the linear current of action repeatedly overcomes lyric retardations. Though enraptured by a stillness beyond time and motion, the lovers, particularly Romeo, have larger obligations to fulfill outside the orchard walls where Mercutio and Tybalt are impatient to die, the Prince to deliver his banishment speech, the apothecary to lay out his quick drugs. With all the play and players waiting for Romeo (and metadramatically for Shakespeare) he can hardly linger forever with Juliet.

Though all the scenes mentioned earlier are lyric in their attempts to set up self-sustaining moments of expressive feeling, the surrender of lyric to drama is especially evident in 3.5. We considered this scene earlier as an instance of the lyric style desperately seeking and failing to impose love's longings on nature and time. In the present connection I would stress the lyric *form* of this lovers' parting since in it Shakespeare scrupulously observes all the conventions of the aubade.[11] Thus when the lovers are compelled to part, a traditional lyric form is "parted" also — in the sense both of being interrupted and more important of being relegated from a lyric whole to a dramatic part. The clear implication is that lyric cannot remain sufficient unto itself in drama but like the lovers themselves must be sacrificed to a larger conception of form.

VII

Yet there is a sense in which Shakespeare has tried to give with one hand and take with the other, which after all is the nature of a sacrifice, something won through losing. What he loses, it would appear, is the permanence, fixity, and stillness of lyric; but what he gains is perhaps a greater stillness, that of dramatic form. This is the rushing stasis, the ever-never species of stillness. For all the rush and bustle of action, the hasty mistimings, the voyaging to eternity are locked perpetually in what is at this stage of his career Shakespeare's most carefully plotted and symmetrically patterned play. As if in reaction to the formlessness of *Love's Labour's Lost*, where he invented a plot that was little more than a series of verbal events brought to an abrupt and frustrate conclusion, he next turned to the preestablished plot of Arthur Brooke's *Tragical Historye of Romeus and Juliet*. Though he trimmed most of the suet from Brooke's plump poem of some 6000 lines, compressing the action and tightening the time scheme, he nonetheless followed the main course of its plot with considerable fidelity.

In *Romeo and Juliet* then Shakespeare knew exactly where he was going. No doubt he did so in other plays too — but here he takes pains to announce his formal mastery of his materials and sense of direction, as for instance in the unusual (at this stage of his

11   These conventions are conveniently listed by R. E. Kaske in "The Aube in Chaucer's *Troilus*," which appears in *Chaucer Criticism: Troilus and Criseyde and the Minor Poems*, ed. Richard J. Schoeck and Jerome Taylor (South Bend, Ind., 1961), pp. 167–179. However, the conventions are perfectly exemplified in the first sixty-five lines of the present scene, to which I therefore refer the curious reader insufficiently up on his aubes.

career) device of the sonnet prologues to Acts 1 and 2, both of which sum up and forecast action. Take the opening prologue:

> Two households, both alike in dignity,
> In fair Verona where we lay our scene,
> From ancient grudge break to new mutiny
> Where civil blood makes civil hands unclean.
> From forth the fatal loins of these two foes
> A pair of star-crossed lovers take their life,
> Whose misadventured piteous overthrows
> Doth with their death bury their parents' strife.
> The fearful passage of their death-marked love
> And the continuance of their parents' rage
> Which, but their children's end, nought could remove,
> Is now the two hours' traffic of our stage;
> The which if you with patient ears attend,
> What here shall miss, our toil shall strive to mend.

The journey metaphor later to be associated primarily with Romeo is here assigned to both lovers in "misadventured," perhaps in "children's end," clearly in "the fearful passage of their death-marked love." Some of that metaphor's linear movement carries over into the following line — "And the continuance of their parents' rage" — so that "continuance" evokes spatial motion as well as temporal duration. Children's love and parental hate both voyage through the play toward the terminal port of death. Then finally the metaphor expands to encompass the presentation of the play itself, fusing temporal and spatial progress in the "two hours' traffic of our stage" figure. For two hours audience and actors are stationed in one theatrical place, and yet as the prologue to Act 3 of *Henry V* puts it —

> our swift scene flies
> In motion of no less celerity
> Than that of thought.

More important than this kind of stationary movement in the theater are the implications of Shakespeare's metadramatic merger of the play's internal fiction, the voyage of the lovers, and the play itself, the traffic of drama ("traffic" appropriately smuggling a commercial connotation into the concept of voyaging). The lovers' voyage occurs under the stars (it is most fittingly a disaster, *dés* + *astre*), which may be considered as both astrological and astronomical influences. Astrologically the stars are equivalent to fate, the fore-plotted journey of star-crossed lovers. And indeed the course of the lovers' voyage and of Shakespeare's play (dramatic traffic) has been pre-plotted in Arthur Brooke's tragical historye. Appropriately, since *fatum* means the "sentences" of the gods, fate has here a literary dimension, and Romeo is quite right to address the dead Paris as "One writ with me in sour misfortune's book" (5.3.82). His journey and that of all the other characters are fated not merely by "inauspicious stars" (5.3.111) but by their literary analogue, an inauspicious plot adopted from Brooke.

From a metadramatic as opposed to thematic standpoint then the repeated references throughout the play to stars, fate, fortune, the curse of birth, the charted journey, all the deterministic forces bearing on the lovers, testify to the sovereignty not merely of cosmic design in human affairs but of plot and form in the construction of *Romeo and Juliet*.[12] And here too is stationary movement. The great haste of the play, the fractious encounters, the stumbling of those who run fast, the recurrent thrusting of the lovers out of the still stasis of lyric, the ramrodding of time — all this activity is necessitated by a plot that demands movement to perfect its design, to complete the voyage of which it is the chart. As chart or plot the dramatic voyage is still, yet nevertheless contains sequences of evolving actions. Its correlative in the fictional world within the play is the fixed pattern of stars that astrologically "moves" the lovers whose unalterable destiny is to advance to the destination of death.[13]

12 Stressing the metadramatic implications of fate is in line with the last paragraph of chapter 9 of *The Poetics* where Aristotle (as Kenneth Burke notes in *Language as Symbolic Action*, Berkeley, Calif., 1966, p. 30) "seems to be saying in effect: The way to make a plot effective is to make it seem inevitable, and the way to make it seem wonderful is to make its imitation of inevitability seem fate-driven." Fate, free will, necessity, and other crucial matters of belief about reality are from the standpoint of poetics merely so much grist for the dramatist's mill.

13 In the ambiguousness of these astrological/astronomical stars we may also see figured the paradox of fatality and free will in dramatic characters.

Not only does Shakespeare forecast his control of dramatic form in the sonnet prologues; he reaffirms it at the end of the play when Friar Laurence, a major manipulator of plot, recapitulates all that has happened (5.3.229–269). At the corresponding point in *Love's Labour's Lost* Shakespeare advertised a failure of dramatic form by allowing Mercade his destructive entrance. Now, however, the friar presents us with a scrupulously detailed forty-line synopsis that accounts for each phase of the action in terms of a governing literary design. In effect the friar pleads his case on the grounds of a coherent plot — not of course his own plot, which failed, but Shakespeare's plot, which succeeds by means of the friar's failure and the lovers' misfortune.

VIII

Shakespeare's success in *Romeo and Juliet* is impressive by comparison with past failures but by no means total. His concentration on, almost celebration of, dramatic form imparts to the play a highly rigid structure based on the division between Montagues and Capulets and between lovers and society. As Sigurd Burckhardt has observed, the play has "a symmetry which, even though it is a symmetry of conflict, is comforting." [14] For despite the family feud the social order is in no real danger of collapse. What turbulence there is gets expressed within a stabilizing framework formed by the Prince and the friar, the one devoted to civil order,

Astrologically the lovers are fated to do what they indeed do, to make their dramatic voyage from *a* to *z*, as any literary character is fated to comply with the dictates of the plot in which he finds himself. But if on the other hand we think of the stars as astronomical guides to navigation, they point up the appearance of self-determination in the characters since as navigator man uses stars instead of being astrologically used by them. Combining the two concepts in one symbol as Shakespeare has done gives us man the navigator using the stars to maintain a pre-charted course from which he cannot deviate. Metadramatically the playwright seeks to maintain the appearance of freedom in his characters, to present them to us as free agents who choose the plot (character issuing in action, as A. C. Bradley put it) that has in literary fact chosen them. "Is it even so?" Romeo says on hearing of Juliet's supposed death, "Then I defy you, stars!" And then on the authority of private feeling and personal volition he rushes back to Verona to keep an appointment in the tomb that Shakespeare's plot had long ago "prescribed" for him.

14 In "The King's Language: Shakespeare's Drama as Social Discovery."

the other all reason and moderation. The virulence of the conflict between families is mitigated by the principals themselves, the spindle-shanked and slippered old men who allow the feud to continue less from rancor than from apathy. And the lovers are themselves untainted by the enmities abroad; they are not at odds with an antagonistic society so much as they are simply apart from it — hurt by ricochet rather than direct intent, by a secret that always could be made public but never is. Hence there is a strong sense of the arbitrary about the play and the lovers' fate, which with all its dependence on accident, coincidence, and sheer mistiming seems imposed and gratuitous. Finally at the end there is a too easy resolution both of the social problem of uniting the families and of the dramatic dilemma of finding a style in which the private and public dimensions of language are happily joined.

For the dramatic or more precisely linguistic dilemma is resolved at the end not stylistically but symbolically, by means of the emblematic statues in which Shakespeare has sought to comprise both private and public values. If the lovers' nominalistic conception of speech implies a verbal purity bordering on nonspeech, here in the silence of the statues is that stillness; and if their love has aspired to a lyric stasis, here too in the fixity of plastic form is that stillness. But by being publicly available — representing the lovers and their value but representing them for the Veronese audience — the statues surpass the aspirations and expressive aims of the lovers. The communicative gap between the private secret love and the social order oblivious to the existence of that love is bridged — and this seems the major significance of the statues — by *artistic form*. Cast in such form, the worth of unique experience is popularized without being cheapened. By shifting from a verbal to a visually symbolic plane Shakespeare ingeniously makes the most of his stylistic liabilities while acknowledging silently that the too pure language of the lovers could not in itself effect such a union.[15] For the

15 In Brooke's poem there are no statues and no gold, only a tomb raised aloft on every side of which in memory of the lovers "were set and eke beneath/ Great store of cunning epitaphs." That Shakespeare has eliminated mention of the epitaphs further emphasizes the nonverbal expressiveness of the statues and hence aligns them with the plastic or spatial aspects of Shake-

dual stillness of the statues, their silence and motionlessness, reflects not merely the poetic tendencies of the lovers but in a large sense the formal properties of Shakespeare's play. The statues materialize at the conclusion, that is, precisely at the point at which the play as temporal experience materializes into spatial form for its audience, the point at which form completes itself on stage and crystallizes in our memories. If language has not linked the public and private world, then form does. And seen in the perspective of dramatic form, the division between lovers and social order is not divisive because the principle of division itself, the playing off of the two worlds in opposition, gives rise to the form of *Romeo and Juliet*. The paradox of form is like that of love in "The Phoenix and the Turtle":

> Two distincts, division none:
> Number there in love was slain.

So the most fruitful coalescence of divided worlds is not to be found in the verbal paradoxes of the oxymoron but in the dramatic paradoxes of the play as shaped entity. As symbols of that shaping the statues of the closing scene reflexively comment on Romeo's oxymorons of the opening scene (1.1.181ff). Those oxymorons clashingly connect the two divided spheres of the opening scene, the public quarrel in the streets and Romeo's private dotage on Rosaline. Hence they are uttered just at the moment when Romeo and Benvolio, who have been talking of Romeo's private problems in love, arrive at the place where the street violence occurred. The "airy word" that bred the "civil brawls" (1.1.96) now expresses in the discordance of Romeo's oxymorons the inner brawling of Petrarchan dotage and unites the two spheres of experience, public and private, as versions of a kind of linguistic noise. In both areas the word has gone bad. Though somewhat redeemed by the speech of the lovers later on, the word never gets placed in public circulation. It is left for the statues to symbolize in form an ideal

speare's dramatic art. Brooke's poem incidentally appears in volume I of Geoffrey Bullough's *Narrative and Dramatic Sources of Shakespeare* (London and New York, 1957) and somewhat abridged in Alice Griffin's *The Sources of Ten Shakespearean Plays* (New York, 1966).

but dramatically unrealized social and verbal union. "Fain would I dwell on form" Juliet told Romeo; but it is really Shakespeare who has dwelt on form in this play, and by doing so has enabled Romeo and Juliet to dwell permanently *in* form.

One final point. I spoke earlier about the nominalistic impulse behind Shakespeare's creation of lovers from whom all family or universal relationships have been deleted — nominalistic because we are asked to confront the lovers as unique particulars. The fact, however, that the lovers are less singular in language and character than we might wish suggests that this deletion of universals is actually antinominalistic, less Aristotelean or Scotist than Platonic. Uniqueness, Shakespeare seems to have realized by the end of this play, is not the condition of being free from universal ties and tendencies; it is not a kind of pure essence left behind after we have burned off all accidental impurities. Distillation of that sort, in fact, leaves us with something very like Platonic universals themselves. But this seems to have been the process by which the lovers were created — a purification by dramatic fiat, giving us a Platonic conception of pure love cast in the role of particulars. At the end of the play, however, Shakespeare seems to sense that with men as with poems uniqueness resides in the form or contextual organization of non-unique qualities — a form sufficiently complex in its internal relations to defy reductive abstraction. Is this not part of the meaning of the statues also? Only by destroying the formal context of the statues can one commercialize the gold of which they are made. Detached though they are from their fictional surroundings, Romeo and Juliet, like the gold in the statues, are permanently embedded in the context of *Romeo and Juliet*, where presumably not even the critic's chisels can get at their priceless worth.

V

A Midsummer Night's Dream

ART'S ILLUSORY SACRIFICE

AT THE end of *Romeo and Juliet* the problem of uniting the lovers not merely to one another but to society as well is resolved in terms of dramatic form, the playwright's contextual bonding agent. The truth and value of young love are given public expression not through language but by being incorporated symbolically into the commemorative gold statues to be erected by the grieving parents. Despite the public feud the lovers' disaster remains a private one. The social order will close around a singular loss, a love of which it had known nothing, toward which it could bear no malice. The burden of failure lies with the lovers, for whom the silence, motionlessness, and eternality of death are preferable to the complex adjustments of speech and conduct required to negotiate with the world outside the orchard wall and the tomb. Out of this private failure, however, Shakespeare carves the successful public shape of his play, in which, as in the gold statues, the lovers find an "everlasting rest."

In *Romeo and Juliet* the structural slackness and verbal waste of *Love's Labour's Lost* are schooled in the economies of artful form. In its closed symmetrical pattern, we may even claim, there is an assured and studied neatness that bespeaks a victory of art over materials rather too submissive to begin with, as in the social union at the end we find the restoration of an order that was never convincingly threatened (as it is, say, in the tragedies to come). The placement of temporary disorder within a protective envelope of art and social order that seals all issues at the end occurs also in *A Midsummer Night's Dream*. Where earlier we had lovers danger-ously set between feuding families that were themselves enclosed by the sane sovereignty of the Prince, we now have lovers imme-diately threatened by Egeus and Puck in their respective realms but ultimately sheltered by the overruling figures of Theseus and Oberon, whose authority restores all. Within this larger frame the comic resolution at the end can be total. The disparate worlds of nobles, workmen, and fairies are united in festivity, and dissension and alienation fade into wisps of half-remembered dreams. Mari-tally, socially, artistically, the knot is tied. With love's labor so well won, nothing seems lost. In *Romeo and Juliet* the victory of form, the bridging of the gap between private love and public order, the restoration of reason to a society lapsed in passion, cost the lovers their lives. Yet here the Theseus principle of rational order seems at the end to be fully confirmed; everybody gets home free, and a spirit of complacency is in the ascendant.

In fact the ease and grace with which it is all done may invite a certain condescension not unlike that of Theseus toward the fairy world. Criticism of *A Midsummer Night's Dream* has on the whole followed the contrasting leads of Theseus and Hippolyta in their responses to the lovers' story of the night. From the standpoint of cool reason Theseus dismisses the lovers' story as an amusing and rather charming instance of strong imagination playing tricks with reality. From a similar standpoint Samuel Pepys dismisses the prod-uct of Shakespeare's imagination as "the most insipid ridiculous play that ever I saw in my life"; and one kind of modern critic — Pepys "translated" into the twentieth century — finds it "barely more than a delicate, tenuous piece of decoration" quite unworthy of critical discussion. On this view we can at best give our rather arch approval to the elegance of the play's verse, the symmetrical disposition of its worlds, and the graceful unfolding of its move-ments while at the same time, in the flintier portions of our soul, endorsing Theseus's "I never may believe/ These antique fables nor these fairy toys" (5.1.2–3).

With a more willing suspension of disbelief, however, other critics find themselves able to agree with Hippolyta that "all the story of the night told over/ . . . grows to something of great constancy" (5.1.23–26). They may for instance "assume that it is a play of marked intellectual content" and that "the variety of the plot is a reflection of an elaborate and ingenious thematic development." Far from being composed of airy nothing the play is distinguished from earlier comedies by the fact that Shakespeare's "matter has now acquired a more searching significance for life, and a closer bearing on the facts of existence." [2] Scaled to this judgment the weightiest matter of the play may be that highly malleable Neoplatonic substance, in which case we witness the spiritual escalation of love from the basement of mere physical attraction toward the recognition of heavenly beauty and virtue,[3] or observe the transformative powers of love-blindness as they project the lovers downward into "irrational animalism" and Bottom upward to a stunning vision of Christian grace.[4] Or again, from a less doctrinaire perspective, we may take the play simply as Shakespeare's assertion that "this world of sense in which we live is but the surface of a vaster unseen world by which the actions of men are affected or overruled." [5]

This modern division of criticism into Theseus and Hippolyta camps had its sixteenth-century anticipation in the dispute between Bellisario Bulgarini and Giacopo Mazzoni over poetry and dreams.[6]

1   Frank Kermode, "The Mature Comedies," in *Early Shakespeare*, vol. 3 of Stratford-upon-Avon Studies, ed. John Russell Brown and Bernard Harris (London, 1961), p. 214.

2   H. B. Charlton, *Shakespearian Comedy* (London, 1938), p. 104.

3   John Vyvyan, *Shakespeare and Platonic Beauty* (New York, 1961), pp. 77–91.

4   Frank Kermode, "The Mature Comedies," p. 219.

5   Harold Goddard, *The Meaning of Shakespeare*, vol. 1 (Chicago, 1951), p. 74.

6   See Baxter Hathaway's account in *The Age of Criticism: The Late Renaissance in Italy* (Ithaca, N.Y., 1962), pp. 355–389.

Bulgarini demoted Dante's "vision" Theseus-like to the status of mere dream and as an advocate of icastic imitation dismissed dream as an unfit subject of poetic representation because it lacks correlatives outside the imagination. Airy nothing, according to him, had no business taking up local habitation and a name in poetry. With something of Hippolyta's liberality, however, Mazzoni argued that dreams are not all that airy, that they have a kind of constancy howsoever strange and admirable, and that in any event they are fit materials for poems since both arise from the same imaginative faculty, dreams being nighttime poems and poems daytime dreams. If so, Bulgarini felt, all the worse for poetry, which should be tethered to intellect and present truth directly, not through moonshiny stories of midsummer nights.[7]

Confronted by such variant opinions both before and after the literary fact, we might well feel that Shakespeare like Bottom has "had a dream past the wit of man to say what dream it was" (4.1.209). We should surely take warning in any event from Bottom's next line: "Man is but an ass if he go about to expound this dream." But unfortunately it is the critic's business to go about expounding dreams, even at the professional risk of growing "marvellous hairy about the face." Still, if we consider the play as a phase of Shakespeare's exploration of the nature, function, and value of dramatic art, something of metadramatic constancy may emerge. Smitten with critical hubris one might hope to find for Shakespeare's play an answer to Theseus's question about the workmen's play: "How shall we find the concord of this discord?" Finding that concord might mean finding a way to reconcile the

7 I am not suggesting that Shakespeare was directly indebted to Bulgarini and Mazzoni in this play, though of course their works were probably never long out of his pocket. Googe's translation of Marcellus Palingenius's *Zodiake of Life* might have done well at his elbow, and Montaigne's essay "On the Power of the Imagination" was also about, well stocked with instruction on the effects of imagination on impotence and flatulence, but on art, alas, nothing. In a fine book on the play (*Something of Great Constancy*, New Haven, Conn., 1966) David Young supplies an excellent review of Elizabethan attitudes toward the concept of imagination (see his chapter on "Bottom's Dream").

claims of reason and imagination, art and reality, Theseus and Hippolyta, and perhaps even Bulgarini and Mazzoni.

II

If Oberon and Theseus are both figures of order, they go about their work in different ways, Oberon specializing in the arts of illusion as befits an illusion and Theseus devoting himself to social rituals as befits a prince. Let me work toward their differences by way of their resemblances, especially as regards the notion of order between the sexes, about which they are both much concerned and one of them sorely vexed.

In affairs of love Theseus has a normative role in the play; his marriage to Hippolyta, the preparations for which structurally bracket the trials of the young lovers, operates as the social ideal against which other relationships are measured. The comic tone of the play and its stress on social rituals naturally preclude a Theseus of full heroic stature. The slayer of Sciron, the Crommyonian sow, and the Cretan minotaur must give way to the exemplar of civil order, justice, and moderation. There is, however, an echo of a less temperate past in Oberon's questioning reminder to Titania:

> Didst thou not lead [Theseus] through the glimmering night
> From Perigenia, whom he ravished?
> And make him with fair Ægle break his faith,
> With Ariadne and Antiopa?   (2.1.77–80)

Theseus has seen his share of the "glimmering light" and revealed an inconstancy of the sort we are to witness in Demetrius and Lysander. But if his infidelities forecast theirs, his courtship of Hippolyta also forecasts the direction their love will take, from apparent hatred and warfare to devotion and peace:

> Hippolyta, I wooed thee with my sword
> And won thy love doing thee injuries.
>   (1.1.16–17)

By reminding us of this peculiar courtship and of Hippolyta's past Shakespeare calls on the familiar Renaissance view of Theseus as the man who righted an imbalance in nature, compelling the Amazonian queen to be true to her sex by becoming subordinate to his, thereby reestablishing the proper hierarchical relationship between man and woman.[8]

This theme reappears of course in fairyland where we find Titania rebelling against Oberon's authority. "Am not I thy lord?" he plaintively protests (2.1.63); but although she acknowledges herself his lady, still

> she perforce withholds the loved boy,
> Crowns him with flowers and makes him all her joy.
> And now they never meet in grove or green,
> By fountain clear or spangled starlight sheen
> But they do square.
> (2.1.26–30)

The point seems to be that Titania is violating natural order both by making the changeling child "all her joy" at the expense of Oberon and by refusing to let the boy pass from a feminine into a masculine world where he belongs if natural growth is to have its way.[9] Thus in demonstrating his power over Titania by causing her to dote on Bottom and surrender the boy to him, Oberon is doing essentially what Theseus did when he conquered Hippolyta.

Oberon exercises a similar influence on the lovers. In the forest the rejected but dogged Helena tells Demetrius

> Your wrongs do set a scandal on my sex.
> We cannot fight for love, as men may do.
> We should be wooed and were not made to woo.
> (2.1.240–242)

Observing this inversion of sexual roles, Oberon sets about restoring order:

> Ere he do leave this grove
> Thou shalt fly him and he shall seek thy love.
> (2.1.245–246)

---

8 Paul A. Olson supplies all the medieval and Renaissance authorities for this in "*A Midsummer Night's Dream* and the Meaning of the Court Marriage," *ELH*, 24(1957):95–119, as well as commenting at length on matrimonial disorder in fairyland.

9 C. L. Barber, *Shakespeare's Festive Comedy* (Princeton, N.J., 1959), p. 137.

And so it falls out, though not without "all this derision" caused by Puck's mistaking Lysander for Demetrius — derision involving the breakdown and readjustment of sexual relations pointed out by C. L. Barber.[10] When the confusion is at its greatest Helena tries to enlist Hermia's support by calling up memories of their "schooldays' friendship" and "childhood innocence":

> So we grew together
> Like to a double cherry, seeming parted
> But yet an union in partition . . .
> And will you rend our ancient love asunder
> To join with men in scorning your poor friend?
> It is not friendly, 'tis not maidenly —
> Our sex as well as I may chide you for it
> Though I alone do feel the injury.
>
> (3.2.208–219)

Puck's "western flower" acts both as a dissolvent on the natural homosexuality of schooldays' friendship, rending "ancient love asunder," and as a catalyst hastening the girls' transition to adult heterosexuality. In an unheroic and domestic form the girls' experience thus mirrors the passage of Hippolyta from her Amazonian past to her Athenian present.

Under the direction of Oberon then, Titania is brought properly to heel and the lovers are paired off in a manner that proves acceptable to Theseus. The movement is from asymmetry to symmetry, from division to unity, from the forest fantastic to the rationally real. But just how is the transition made? What makes Theseus, the Theseus who in the opening act is absolute for law, blandly dismiss Egeus's demands in the fourth act ("I beg the law,

10 *Ibid.*, pp. 129–130. Incidentally Mr. Barber has written so persuasively about this play that it is puzzling to find him saying that there is "the confident assumption dominant in *A Midsummer Night's Dream* that substance and shadow can be kept separate," which he feels accounts for "the peculiarly unshadowed gaiety of the fun [the play] makes with fancy" (p. 161). As I have already suggested, I find the interpenetrations of shadow and substance, illusion and reality, both manifold and somewhat baffling — at any rate easily kept separate only by a Theseus-like rationalism that an insightful and imaginative critic such as Barber goes well beyond — and a bit further on I'll urge that there are sobering bases to the gay and fanciful structure of the play.

the law, upon his head") and send Hermia off to the temple to be married instead of to a nunnery to contemplate the cold chaste moon? The imaginative transformations that Oberon has wrought in the forest Theseus confirms in the palace and temple, which would seem to suggest a final union between imagination and reason. But Theseus places his own rational construction on what it is he confirms. There is no room in that construction for dream or drama, let alone fairy kings and their devious doings, and yet it is by the route of dream, drama, and fairy that the lovers make their way into Theseus's good graces and Athens's social order.

III

This stress on order — the reestablishment of sexual hierarchies and the whole movement of the play toward the binding unity of triple marriages — implies a tidiness of artistic form that leaves the play discretely boxed off from Pepys's reality and Bulgarini's truth. Countering this closed order of art, however, is an open-endedness that enables art, rather like Hermione's metamorphosing statue in *The Winter's Tale*, to unfold into reality. The internal fiction of the drama not only mirrors but actually merges with the theatrical occasion, and the division between art and actuality vanishes. If we remember that the play was probably written and first performed as part of the festivities attending an aristocratic wedding (that of Elizabeth de Vere to the Earl of Derby on January 26, 1595, is most frequently proposed) then it becomes evident that Shakespeare's first audience in the manor house was insinuated into an imaginative identification with the audience of Bottom's play as the entertainment honoring Theseus and Hippolyta became not just analogous to but literally part of the entertainment provided by Shakespeare's play for the unknown couple whose marriage was being celebrated.[11] In view of the pronounced influence of the masque on the play's structure, it is also highly likely that at that first performance the dance called for by Oberon (5.1.403) fea-

11 In "*A Midsummer Night's Dream* and the Wedding Guests," *Shakespeare Quarterly*, 4(1953):139-144, Paul N. Siegel discusses the structure of the play in the light of the occasion of its first performance.

tured the "taking out" of members of the audience in the conventional masque manner.[12] And after the dance, when Oberon says

> With this field-dew consecrate
> Every fairy take his gait
> And each several chamber bless,
> Through this palace, with sweet peace
>
> (5.1.422–425)

it seems equally likely as a final charming touch that the fairies left the stage and passed through each several chamber of the manor house that served as Shakespeare's temporary theater and as Theseus's "palace." The fictional blessing would thus pass uninterruptedly into an actual blessing in which the "field-dew" of artistic illusion consecrates reality. In this way the play's openness of form serves the comic theme of social inclusiveness with wonderful felicity, the world of comedy expanding beyond the borders of its own fiction to enfold and absorb the social world of an Elizabethan marriage party.

It is not merely in the masquelike aspects of the play, especially at the end, that Shakespeare urges the interpenetration of art and reality. Under the influence of ubiquitous moonlight the borders between dream, drama, and waking reality deliquesce and all three circulate together in strange solution. Seeking to translate himself from weaver into Pyramus during the rehearsal of the workmen's play, Bottom finds himself transported right on through the illusions of drama into a fairyland reality which, when he makes his return journey to the cold hillside of perturbed reason, dissolves into dream. The lovers emerge from the nightmare experience of the forest glancing apprehensively back "with parted eye/ When everything seems double," still uncertain whether they wake or sleep. And in the epilogue Puck invites the audience to take the title of the play in full literalness and translate the dramatic experience into mere dream. Beneath the neatly differentiated Apollonian images of literary form in the theater — the rational sharpness of outline

12 For the influence of the masque on the play see Enid Welsford's *The Court Masque: A Study in the Relationship between Poetry and the Revels* (Cambridge, 1927), pp. 331–332.

that separates not only bears from bushes in Theseus's well-ordered world (5.1.22) but art's fantasies from life's facts as well — runs the unindividuated flow of Dionysian dream.[13]

This indistinctness of form and outline lends the lovers' experiences in the forest a mythic aspect. For instance, Ernst Cassirer says of the mythopoeic primitive mind: "Its view of life is a synthetic, not an analytic one [as in scientific thought]. Life is not divided into classes and subclasses. It is felt as an unbroken continuous whole which does not admit of any clean-cut and trenchant distinctions. . . . Nothing has a definite, invariable, static shape. By a sudden metamorphosis everything may be turned into everything. If there is any characteristic and outstanding feature of the mythical world, any law by which it is governed — it is this law of metamorphosis."[14] An excellent description of the fairy-forest world.

This principle of metamorphosis operates also in the dream world, and in this midsummer night's dream it goes by the name "translation." What in the dream drama is metamorphosis or translation is in poetry "metaphor," by which in Cassirer's phrase "everything may be turned into everything" or, as Northrop Frye puts it, "everything is potentially identical with everything else."[15] The "scientific" mind of Theseus would separate asses from Bottoms and at most perhaps apply a simile, "Bottom is like an ass," whereas the poetic imagination not only employs metaphors but may even claim an identity between tenor and vehicle by setting on Bottom's shoulders the genuine apple-munching ear-twitching article. Not just in particulars like this but in its general breakdown of the barriers between dream, art, myth, historical periods, and inner and outer nature (the forest within and without) Shakespeare's play repeatedly asserts the imaginative unity of all disparates that Cassirer associates with the myth-minded.

13 I know that Nietzsche associates dream with Apollo and ritual integration with Dionysus, but Shakespeare's prophetic imagination is capacious enough in this play to accommodate Freud as well as Nietzsche.

14 *An Essay on Man*, in the Doubleday Anchor Books Edition (New York, 1956), p. 108.

15 *Anatomy of Criticism* (Princeton, N.J., 1957), p. 124.

My present concern, however, is not myth but metadrama, which specializes in its own forms of dissolution and transformation. In the epilogue, for instance, Puck humorously tells the audience that if they like they can reverse the creative movement from dream to art by imagining that their theatrical experience of *A Midsummer Night's Dream* has been merely a midsummer night's dream. Here is the "uncreating word" of Pope's goddess of Dulness wielded with a vengeance. However, Puck's suggestion merely confirms an interchangeability of dream and drama implied elsewhere in the play. For instance, though in retrospect the lovers' forest experience seems to them a nightmarish dream, while it is in process it bears the likeness of drama — so much so that we may claim to have in a sense two plays within the play. One is the actual play in which Bottom and crew act the roles of noble lovers, and of a few stage properties as well; the other is a metaphoric play in which the young lovers figure as unwitting actors in a drama produced, directed, and acted in by Oberon and Puck. Regarding Oberon as a kind of interior dramatist is in keeping with Theseus's patronizing remark about the workmen actors, "The best in this kind are but shadows" (5.1.213), since Oberon according to Puck is "king of shadows" (3.2.347) — a royal role that can be assigned also to the playwright Shakespeare, whose commands to his subjects take the form of the script that rules his actors. Oberon and Puck are analogous not only to playwright and players but to the audience as well. Thus as Lysander and Helena approach, Puck asks Oberon "Shall we their fond pageant see?" (3.2.114), which echoes the statement Puck made on encountering Bottom's company in rehearsal:

> What, a play toward? I'll be an auditor —
> An actor too perhaps if I see cause.
>   (3.1.81–82)

Consummate actor that he is, he sees cause to take a part in both Bottom's play and the lovers' drama. Bottom, who is unalterably Bottom, wants to act all the parts in his play. Puck, who is mercurially Puck and therefore anything he wishes — he can neigh "in likeness of a filly foal," take the "very likeness of a roasted crab," or assume the shape of a "three-foot stool" (2.1.46ff) — does not play all the parts in the lovers' drama, only those of Lysander and Demetrius as Oberon bids him:

> Like to Lysander sometime frame thy tongue,
> Then stir Demetrius up with bitter wrong;
> And sometime rail thou like Demetrius.
>
> (3.2.360–362)

If we accept these various cues and regard the story of the night as the "drama" of the night, then the breakdown of sexual relationships noted earlier becomes part of a general dissolving of past identities analogous to the actor's submerging of personal identity in a fictional role (especially when it is a boy actor adopting a feminine role). "Am not I Hermia? Are not you Lysander?" (3.2.273). Apparently not — no more than John Heminges as Lysander is still John Heminges, though of course the acting of the lovers is involuntary.[16] Helena had earlier wished to give up everything if only she could be "translated" into Hermia (1.1.191); and in the forest that is precisely what happens, both men now loving her with the same devotion they had once accorded Hermia, though she believes them to be "counterfeiting" (as indeed they are in one sense). Transfers of roles and identities are general: Hermia becomes translated into Helena and learns how it feels to be scorned; Lysander plays the Demetrius who once loved Helena; and Demetrius ultimately plays his former self by loving Helena again and permanently. From this standpoint the lovers' experience in the forest is more genuinely dramatic than the carefully rehearsed and formally presented *Pyramus and Thisbe* since the

16 In terms of the metaphor of drama anyhow it is involuntary; but as dream behavior their conduct in the forest is at least partly voluntary, representing as it would a release of inner impulse and desire, a psychodramatic exploration of fancies and fears that must go unexpressed in the rational world of Theseus, who plays ego to Egeus's superego and Puck's puckish id. Associating dream illusions with those of drama is hardly novel in Shakespeare. One may think of Prospero's dream-drama illusions, of Hamlet wondering on the performance of a player who "in a fiction, a dream of passion" could act thus and so, or nearer to home of Christopher Sly drifting like his spiritual cousin Bottom mystified between dream and drama.

identities of the lovers are indeed lost in their imposed roles whereas the great failure of *Pyramus and Thisbe* is its actors' inability to act, to lose their identities even imaginatively in fictional roles. By remaining obtrusively present and "untranslated" in *Pyramus and Thisbe*, reality destroys the dramatic fiction — the actors devour the characters as it were — whereas the fiction of the forest drama swallows up and digests reality.

What the fiction of the forest digests reality into is comedy, though not quite the "Lamentable Comedy" that that proto-Polonius and theorist of genre Quince labels his play. The comic movement of this forest play is through the disintegration of its fictional society in "all this derision" to a reformation of it in a happy ending as everyone is united in sleep and love under the same greenwood tree — a social union as paradoxically harmonious as the cries of the Spartan hounds Hippolyta refers to just before the sleeping lovers are found: "I never heard/ So musical a discord, such sweet thunder" (4.1.121–122). The power of illusion that translates reality into drama is appropriately not merely that of the flowers Puck employs but that of language too — the word magic of the verbal charms that accompany each of Puck's five applications of the flower juices. In the form of such charms words have considerable power to govern conduct in the forest drama, but they can hardly substitute for a script. Thus the comedy is on the order of commedia dell'arte, each actor improvising his own way ungoverned by a presiding formal structure, so that a comic conclusion is achieved only because the dramatist Oberon, dissatisfied with Puck's bungled directing, assigns him the role of *flora ex machina*. Judging from Berowne's remark in *Love's Labour's Lost* that their sport is not a comedy because "Jack hath not Jill," Puck's last verbal charm serves the cause not only of love but of generic form as well:

> And the country proverb known,
> That every man should take his own,
> In your waking shall be shown.
> Jack shall have Jill,
> Nought shall go ill.
>
> (3.2.458–462)

If Oberon as playwright within the play has created a drama
that is merely illusion and delusion, then perhaps it too deserves the
damnation with faint praise bestowed by Theseus on the workmen's play: "This palpable-gross play hath well beguiled/ The
heavy gait of night" (5.1.374–375). For indeed, palpable-gross
though it is, the workmen's play is insubstantial as any dream, serving only as idle entertainment to ease the hours before its audience
returns to (if it ever really left) untheatrical life and its fictions
melt into thin air. And Shakespeare's fictions, we are bound to
wonder — do they too melt into thin air at the final curtain? So a
good many critics would seem to feel, and so Shakespeare would
seem to suggest by having Puck offer the audience the option of
thinking

> That you have but slumbered here
> While these visions did appear.
> And this weak and idle theme,
> No more yielding but a dream.
>
> (5.1.432–435)

As a disavowal of the relevance of art to life and a surrender of all
claims to dramatic value, this seems almost criminally modest —
rather like the utter frailty Shakespeare ascribes to beauty in Sonnet 65:

> How with this rage [of destroying Time] shall
>   beauty hold a plea,
> Whose action is no stronger than a flower?

Aside from the fact that the action of flowers is very strong indeed in *A Midsummer Night's Dream*, we would want to note that
through Puck Shakespeare is inviting his audience to do precisely
what the lovers did at the end of their forest drama — allow drama
to dwindle into dream and hence to deny any meaningful connection between the story of the night and actual life in Athens. This
parallel, however, puts a very different light on Shakespeare's
modesty since the forest drama not only absorbs reality by transforming the prior identities of the lovers but, more important, car-

ries over into reality in much the same way that Shakespeare's fairy actors pass with their blessings out of Theseus's palace and into each several chamber of the Elizabethan manor house. For the lovers all charms apparently fly at the touch of cold philosophy personified in Theseus. But only apparently. They may admit afterwards that what they experienced while acting in Oberon's and Puck's "play," though vivid and seeming real, was actually no more yielding than a dream ("And by the way let us recount our dreams," 4.1.203); but nonetheless the realignments of love wrought by the dream-drama of the night no more disappear at dawn than, as Oberon assures us, the fairies do (3.2.388ff). From the standpoint of cool reason and known fact Theseus says "I know you two are rival enemies"; but for reasons beyond reason Demetrius and Lysander no longer hate one another, and by some strange power, Demetrius says,

> my love to Hermia
> Melted as is the snow, seems to me now
> As the remembrance of an idle gaud
> Which in my childhood I did dote upon.
>
> (4.1.169–172)

The dramatic illusions of the forest, having created fictional enmities and then dissolved them into general concord, have dissolved the real enmities of the past as well. And in the waking world, through the agency of Theseus's royal command, they even dissolve the hard stuff of law and overbear the will of Egeus, thus enabling the marriage of true minds to be ratified in the temple. In view of the results of the forest drama then, the modesty of Shakespeare's epilogue is transformed by humorous irony into something along these lines: "If it makes you feel more reasonable you can adopt Theseus's attitude and regard the play as no more significant than a dream — at best an amusing way to pass the time. But like the lovers who also converted their experience into dream — an experience in many ways analogous to drama — whether you realize it or not you have experienced something here of enduring value and with a reality of its own."

But what is the enduring value of the play to the audience?

Shakespeare actually seems more concerned to imply the value of the audience to the play. At the end of *Love's Labour's Lost* Rosaline asserted that a "jest's prosperity lies in the ear/ Of him that hears it," a claim that has obvious implications for drama and dramatists, who had better study to deserve well by that ear. More than that though. The playwright must not merely please his audience but enlist its cooperation in the creative process itself. Sometimes in fact the audience may be required to make a major contribution to the creation of drama: Theseus having said that the workmen's play can be amended by imagination, Hippolyta replies "It must be your imagination then, and not theirs" (5.1.216). Like Rosaline's in its context, Hippolyta's remark is excessive: only an audience of heroic imaginative talents could "amend" the workmen's play. Even Shakespeare's play, however, though hardly in need of imaginative amendment, requires imaginative participation by the audience, since any play viewed from the Theseus perspective of "cool reason" – say a demand for total verisimilitude of the sort that brought on the strictest interpretation of the dramatic unities – cannot help declining into absurdity. In *Troilus and Cressida* Ulysses tells the lagging Achilles that however great his physical or spiritual endowments a man

> Cannot make boast to have that which he hath,
> Nor feels not what he owes, but by reflection,
> As when his virtues shining upon others
> Heat them and they retort that heat again
> To the first giver.   (3.3.98–102)

Achilles elaborates:

>   This is not strange, Ulysses.
> The beauty that is borne here in the face
> The bearer knows not, but commends itself
> To others' eyes. Nor doth the eye itself,
> That most pure spirit of sense, behold itself,
> Not going from itself; but eye to eye opposed
> Salutes each other with each other's form.
> For speculation turns not to itself
> Till it hath travelled and is mirrored there
> Where it may see itself.   (3.3.102–111)

The beauty that is borne in dramatic art may also be said to be unknown to the bearer — playwright and actor — until having commended itself to the eyes of an audience it becomes "mirrored there/ Where it may see itself." This courteous nod to the audience is more than courtesy and not just an elaborate way of saying, as in one clever way or another most Shakespearean epilogues do say, "don't sit on your hands." Both virtue and beauty as they apply to persons are the products of a generative intercourse between bearer and observer; and dramatic beauty and value are born of the intercourse between the various imaginations of dramatist, actors, and audience.[17] By this point Shakespeare has come to acknowledge the audience's creative role in the collaborative enterprise of drama; it is no longer regarded as merely a corruptive appetite for sensations that must be catered to as in *Titus Andronicus* or disregarded as in *Love's Labour's Lost*.

But if the audience holds up the mirror to the play, there is a sense in which the play holds up a mirror to the audience also. In a passage quoted by Hugo von Hofmannsthal, Lucian says "When every spectator becomes one with what happens on the stage, when everyone recognises in the performance, as in a mirror, the reflection of his own true impulses, then, but not until then, success has been achieved. Such a dumb spectacle is at the same time nothing less than the fulfilment of the Delphic maxim 'Know thyself,' and those who return from the theatre have experienced what was truly an experience."[18]

17 See in this connection R. W. Dent's "Imagination in *A Midsummer Night's Dream*," *Shakespeare Quarterly*, 15(1964):115–129. The workmen's play, Dent argues, may be taken to imply a kind of Shakespearean poetics to which the concept of imagination is central. The result is "a delightful exposition of the follies produced by excessive imagination in love and the pleasures produced by controlled imagination in art" (p. 128). Dent's position is reinforced on the whole by Norman Rabkin, who in *Shakespeare and the Common Understanding* (New York, 1967) keys on the shifting symbolic values of the moon to argue that Shakespeare "with his characteristic ambivalence [sees art] simultaneously as 'base and vile' yet of the highest 'form and dignity'" (p. 205). J. R. Brown also has a quasi-metadramatic treatment of the play in which he centers his discussion in the play-within-the-play; see his chapter "Love's Truth" in *Shakespeare and His Comedies* (London, 1957).

18 Cited by H. A. Hammelmann in *Hugo von Hofmannsthal* (New Haven, Conn., 1957), p. 35.

A major kind of knowledge made available to its audience by *A Midsummer Night's Dream* is that of the inner forms and impulses of the human mind itself — the tricks and shaping fantasies of strong imagination and the forces directing it but also the range and limits of cool reason. The mind that comes to focus on the play and especially on the drama of the forest comes to focus on itself. Externalized in the illusions of drama, this inner world encountered by the audience appears not in Lucian's mirror of mimetic reproduction but as projected through the prism of artistic imagination, from which it issues in rich and delightful distortion. The very ambiguity of the fairy world, which asks simultaneously to be accepted and rejected, acknowledges the real and compelling force of imaginative impulse while humorously denying the validity of its mythopoeic products. The more rational the existence of Oberon and Titania is made to seem — as in the detailed assertion of a cause and effect relationship between their marital disharmonies and the waywardness of nature (2.1.81–117) — the more illusionary they become. By the same token the surpassing excellence of Puck's mimetic genius nullifies his claims to exist. Oberon, Titania, and Puck are of course folkloristic explanations of otherwise inexplicable events. The fairy king and queen anthropomorphize disorders in nature — forward springs and other seasonal irregularities, windstorm, floods caused by lunar influence (Titania as the moon goddess Cynthia) — while Puck as befits a lesser fairy accounts for domestic mishaps. Embodiments both of human bewilderment and of the rationalizing impulse that it begets, they are especially fit figures to preside over the lovers' collective nightmare, itself brought on by that irrational aberration in human nature and domestic experience, love.

If then the fairies are deities of the psyche and not the sky, symbols of subjective and largely wayward impulses or dramatists of the unconscious, they are also, one needs to add, legitimately "out there" in the fictional world of the play, as much so as Theseus himself. And out there they are bodyings forth of nature's impulses. As usual in Shakespeare, lovers and ordinary people must rediscover the fact that they are subjects in a wider and more fun-

"All world's a stage"

damental state than that of Theseus's Athens before they can be fully civilized, even if that rediscovery seems but a dream. The lovers owe fealty to Nature first, must play their roles in her drama before returning to the more carefully plotted and comforting plays of state. The journey into the forest is a journey both outward to external nature and inward to human nature, both of which coalesce benevolently in the final concord of this discord.

We are not, therefore, invited to accept the fact of fairy but the metaphor of fairy, and not as a metaphor for something like unruly providence, heaven with hellish undertones, or some other supersensory place or power. If Shakespeare is suggesting that "this world of sense in which we live is but the surface of a vaster unseen world" then that unseen world is within rather than outside or above man. The events and characters in the forest present the drama of the dreaming mind whose imaginative impulses are released from reason (though often rationalized in terms of it) and divorced from daytime fact: a particular midsummer night's dream of the lovers (for it is as well as is not their dream) in which the subjective play of love and hate is enacted as drama, but by metaphoric extension the actors', the audience's, Shakespeare's, man's dream too. Dream, in short, becomes drama, a drama in which man sees his dreams.[19]

v

For the translation of dream into drama, language would seem to be crucial. In *Romeo and Juliet*, as we have argued, the gap between the subjective experience of the lovers and the public world of Verona could not be bridged this side of death. The language

19 Or, to put a different construction on it, the audience has experienced the waking dream of art. "Modern criticism," Kenneth Burke has said, "and psychoanalysis in particular, is too prone to define the essence of art in terms of the artist's weaknesses. It is, rather, the audience which dreams, while the artist oversees the conditions which determine this dream. He is the manipulator of blood, brains, heart, and bowels which, while we sleep, dictate the mould of our desires" ("Psychology and Form" from *Counter-Statement*, rev. ed., Los Altos, Calif., 1953, pp. 36–37). Given a conductor of dreams with such absolute dominion over his dreaming subjects as this, Shakespeare's self-deprecating epilogue again takes on a cunning gamesomeness.

that might have served as an agent of communion remained undiscovered; the lovers' speech, too diffident to go abroad in a world of linguistic contagion, kept purely and autonomously to itself and died into silence. A sense of resolution was imparted to the play not through speech but by ushering in the concept of dramatic form as a substitute agent of communion.

Language is less consistently an issue in *A Midsummer Night's Dream*, perhaps because the play was designed initially for viewers of much greater verbal sophistication than those that flocked across Finsbury Fields to the Theatre. But if such an audience offers the playwright certain assurances it also should give him pause. The author of a play specifically commissioned for one evening's entertainment could hardly avoid wondering anew, I should think, about the value and permanence of his art, which by the nature of his assignment seems defined as transient amusement. The one-time occasional play, however, only intensifies an issue of which the dramatist must always be unpleasantly conscious, the fact that his art is born and dies in the same theatrical instant, the curtain closing as efficiently as the tomb. How then does an occasional play, even one for which its author no doubt intends a subsequent life in the theater, transcend the conditions of its brief existence? How does it graduate from evanescent and idle dream to abiding art?

One way it does *not* so graduate is illustrated by Bottom. Awaking from a most rare vision which he has experienced with most ordinary unimaginativeness (as for instance in his conversion of Mustardseed and Cobweb to mustardseed and cobweb, a mythopoesis in reverse) and which in a sense therefore he has not experienced at all, Bottom delivers his famous speech:

> I have had a dream past the wit of man to say what dream it was. Man is but an ass if he go about to expound this dream. Methought I was — there is no man can tell what. Methought I was — and methought I had — but man is but a patched fool if he will offer to say what methought I had. The eye of man hath not heard, the ear of man hath not seen, man's hand is not able to taste, his tongue to conceive, nor his heart to report, what my dream was.   (4.1.209ff)

Beyond sight, hearing, and feeling, Bottom's most rare vision is most of all beyond speech. Contrast Hamlet, who when Gertrude assures him (and herself) that the ghost is but "the very coinage of [his] brain" replies

> It is not madness
> That I have uttered. Bring me to the test
> And I the matter will re-word, which madness
> Would gambol from. (3.4.141–144)

Bottom, however, lacks Hamlet's gift of speech, and because he can neither word nor reword it the "matter" of his fairy experience fades into incommunicable subjectivity, into a wordless "dream past the wit of man to say what dream it was" — and this despite the fact that Bottom "hath simply the best wit of any handicraft man in Athens" (4.2.9–10). Bottom's situation is analogous not only to that of the awakened lovers but to that of the playwright Shakespeare as well. Bottom has in fact an impulse to art, thinking that he will get Peter Quince to write a ballad of his dream. But skilled carpenter that he surely is, Quince, alas, can no more raise a balladic edifice on a bottomless dream than Bottom himself. Bottom does not even try to say what his dream was:

> BOTTOM. Masters, I am to discourse wonders, but ask me not what, for if I tell you, I am no true Athenian. I will tell you everything right as it fell out.
> QUINCE. Let us hear, sweet Bottom.
> BOTTOM. Not a word of me. All I will tell you is that the Duke hath dined. (4.2.29ff)

Bottom figures for us in comic parody the typical human plight, which is perhaps why he is both ridiculous and oddly touching, his mind big and boggling with the unshareable dream of self, longing to discourse wonders for which his language can provide no concrete habitation. Experienced in isolation, his dream is unverifiable and truly "hath no bottom," so that if he tries to express it he will be "no true Athenian" not merely because it would prove him an ass instead but because he would not be believed. As a would-be artist in speech Bottom lacks the wordpower to say what dream it was, the oneirocritical talents to know what dream it was, and an audience of sufficient imaginative flexibility to grasp what dream it was. Not that Bottom's most rare vision has put him in contact with the mysteries of the universe — there has been something too much of that in criticism of the play — but it has at least put him in touch with his own nature and thus provided an opportunity for self-knowledge: "Methought I was — and methought I had — but . . ." But there is no danger that Bottom will experience even a comic anagnorisis: the knowledge does not take, the vision fades into irrecoverable dream, and Bottom hustles off to bray his lines in *Pyramus and Thisbe.*[20]

In Bottom's case, art, lacking the midwife of speech, dies aborning and dream remains merely dream. Only masters of poetic language like Shakespeare and Hamlet can word and reword the matter that seems but airy nothing to Theseuses and Gertrudes. In wording such matter in *A Midsummer Night's Dream* Shakespeare has translated the normally incommunicable subjective dimension of human experience, of which dream is the emblem, into external dramatic form where it becomes publicly available. As public dream the play is like the shared dream of the four lovers in the forest, which unlike Bottom's private dream has a continuing efficacy in the waking world. The dramatic experience in which playwright, actors, and audience all participate, whether in an aristocrat's manor house or the Theatre, thus becomes a kind of secular ritual of communion, with the play itself the focal illusion whose existence and significance are created by a collective imaginative act and whose value lies partly in the fact that it enables a sharing of inner experience otherwise inaccessible. The play and the audience imaginatively unite and mutually transform each other in the act of knowledge. The theatrical experience made possible by the play thus mirrors the fictional experience presented in the play. The wedding of imaginations in the theater, which both creates and is created by the play, mirrors the marriage of true minds cre-

20 I have been a bit ungenerous to Bottom. After all, if his dream primarily exposes his assishness it also sets him beside a fairy queen. There is clearly something of the sacredness of folly about Bottom, the anointed innocent singled out for a kind of grace not despite but because of his doltishness.

ated both by Oberon's forest drama and by *A Midsummer Night's Dream*. Hippolyta's famous lines

> But all the story of the night told over
> And all their minds transfigured so together
> More witnesseth than fancy's images
> And grows to something of great constancy
>
> (5.1.23–26)

apply not only to the forest drama and the lovers' minds but to *A Midsummer Night's Dream* and the collective transfiguration of mind wrought by it in the theater as well. In this sense, far from being airy nothing compared to a world of hard realities beyond the apron, drama actually imposes its most rare vision on that world. As the fairies dance out of fiction and into each several chamber of reality, precisely at the moment that Puck is deprecating the play as mere dream, that would seem to be at least part of the blessing they bestow. The play survives the occasion of its performance not merely by achieving a permanence of form as in *Romeo and Juliet* but by imprinting its illusions in the minds of its audience, where it receives a new and enduring life.

On this view the poet-playwright takes on the role of high priest of subjectivity, presiding over and with the magic of his language and imagination calling forth to public view the mysteries of mind and feeling. Since one of the impulses in Shakespeare's art up to this point has been the lyric withdrawal from the audience into an indwelling privacy — the park in *Love's Labour's Lost*, the orchard in *Romeo and Juliet* — we should take special note of the fact that here it is not the workings of the dramatist's mind that receive expression. The play is not Shakespeare's private dream publicized (Orpheus thrown to the mad maenads of Dionysus or Lavinia surrendered up to the Goths) but rather the audience's dream made public and reexperienced as art. The art is Shakespeare's, but it is art become genuinely dramatic, distanced from self. It is Bottom who sees the drama (rather as Shakespeare saw *Love's Labour's Lost* up until the end) as a constellation of roles and occasions in which he may personally sparkle. Shakespeare like Oberon has the far more demanding task of governing all roles and occasions while remaining personally "invisible" (2.1.186) in a way that would satisfy even Stephen Dedalus's strictures on the dramatic mode. That Shakespeare succeeded in achieving this personal invisibility in this and subsequent plays has been the lament of would-be biographers and the delight of audiences and critics ever since. For the genuine dramatist, it would seem, the private dream is inevitably bottomless, and the poet who attempts to expound such a dream — that is, seeks to use drama as a medium of self-expression, a platform for the direct nonmetaphoric exhibition of feeling and thought — may well become an ass. As Shakespeare now conceives of it, the poet's proper task is to wed the audience to itself through the ceremony of dramatic art, not to stand himself before the altar.

VI

Wedding the audience to itself, however, is a mysterious business not easily brought off, in part because the poet lacks authority for his words and illusions, there being no Holy Church certifying his ceremonies, and in part because the audience may not be anxious to confront its dreaming self, much less enter a world-without-end bargain with it. This is especially likely in view of the nature of the self revealed. For in contrast to Theseus's court where a rational though initially repressive social order is crystallized in law, where individual impulse is kept in check by the principle of hierarchy, and where all the powers of the state are mobilized in the service of stability and security, the forest world of Oberon carries in comic solution certain elements of terror. Even in the opening scene the placid surface of order is roiled, not only by the public dispute promoted by the waspish Egeus but by suggestions of a more fundamental rage against which the beauty of love must hold a plea. For if despite all other obstacles love did flower, then as Lysander says

> War, death, or sickness did lay siege to it,
> Making it momentany as a sound,
> Swift as a shadow, short as any dream,
> Brief as the lightning in the collied night

That in a spleen unfolds both heaven and earth
And ere a man hath power to say "Behold!"
The jaws of darkness do devour it up.
So quick bright things come to confusion.

(1.1.142–149)

For an instant the shadow of *Romeo and Juliet* falls across the play. And indeed in the forest quick bright things do come to confusion and derision. The lovers make the perilous journey of romance beyond the safeguards of society and reason into the realm of nightmare. Former relationships disintegrate; truth, honor, and love metamorphose into falsehood, disloyalty, and malice; and the whole structure of reason and order collapses in absurdity. The effect on all the lovers is summed up in the helpless frustration of Hermia's "I am amazed and know not what to say" (3.2.344).

Nonetheless no audience ever took this as the stuff of potential tragedy because one aspect of the play's blessing is that it provides for the containment of irrationality and chaos. From this standpoint Puck becomes the active agent of a forest drama that raises and purges the wayward human impulses whose release in real life generates terror and pity. Not that Oberon as forest dramatist is shaping his play with the Aristotelian primer in hand or mind. His play's catharsis results not only from the containment of incipient chaos by literary form — Dionysiac pain by Apollonian images — but also from the transformation of the potentially terrifying into high comedy (for instance the fear of loss of self into a delightful comedy of mistaken identities) and from the blurring and distancing of terror through illusion.

The techniques of dramatic containment are of course by no means new to Shakespeare. As early as *3 Henry VI* (2.5) for instance he had used a dramatic ritual marked by ceremonious rhetoric, stylized action, and antiphonal dialogue to contain the presentation of political and social chaos and hence to forecast even in England's darkest moments her ultimate return to unity and order under Henry VII. But whereas in *3 Henry VI* and the histories generally (e.g. *1 Henry VI*, 1.1; *Richard III*, 5.3; *Richard II*, 3.4) this containment is effected by rituals implying religious, political, or social ideals, in the forest drama it is for the first time accomplished entirely in terms of artistic illusion. Suggestions that beneath the surface of ordered, civilized, rational life lies a gulf of meaninglessness or even latent malignity, "jaws of darkness" in wait for true love, are certainly present; but they are triply distanced from the audience, which sees them, in order of recession, as created by Shakespeare's play, by Oberon's and Puck's magic play, and by the dream play of the lovers' minds. Thus to the audience as well as to the lovers afterwards "These things seem small and undistinguishable,/ Like far-off mountains turned into clouds" (4.1.191–192). Perhaps Hermia's remark is even more to the point: "Methinks I see these things with parted eye/ When everything seems double" (4.1.193–194). For there is an unmistakable doubleness about the dream drama of the forest and that of the entire play. Both fuse and yet separate reality and fantasy; both join reason and imagination in an initially disquieting but ultimately beneficent metaphoric union; and both set before their audience images of a nightmare from whose anxieties none of its members is wholly safe, and yet by framing those images in an illusion within an illusion dissolve their threat in laughter. Still the laughter is generated at least in part by the act of self-recognition made possible by the translation of subjective vagueness into the objective clarity of dramatic form, however illusionary its materials.

On the one hand then, as I suggested in the previous section, the play serves as the focal point of a secular ritual of imaginative and emotional communion, causing the theatrical experience itself to become a paradigm of the ideal social order. But this communal marriage within the theater or manor house must be followed by a divorce. The poet as priest, having learned to say "the perfect ceremony of love's rite" (Sonnet 23), must also learn the words and ways to break that bond, for the audience can no more remain locked in art's illusions than the lovers can be left permanently asleep in the forest.[21] In the withdrawal and return movement that

21 In *The Taming of the Shrew*, which may have been written before *A Midsummer Night's Dream*, Shakespeare did not, I think, realize the full implications of this. If he based *The Shrew* on *A Shrew* (which may of course

governs the play's structure, the lovers must be awakened from
Oberon's dream play and reenter Athens, even as Shakespeare's
audience must be returned to London. And reentering Athens
means reentering a world presided over by the rational principle of
hierarchic order.

Had Shakespeare been the naive woodnote warbler of nine-
teenth-century criticism, he might have sought to champion the
poetic imagination by forcing even Theseus to give credence to the
story of the night and by bringing the fairies visibly into the final
scene as part of the audience of the workmen's play, perhaps en-
throning Oberon and Titania beside Theseus and Hippolyta. But
he is less concerned to claim priority for either reason or imagination than to suggest how man arrives at a rational life without for-
feiting the liberating virtues of the imaginative vision. And he is
shrewd enough in the ways of the world to know that the imaginative vision can coexist with the rational life but not, given the self-
gratifying hierarchies of reason, on the same plane. Oberon will always be invisible to Theseus, though what Oberon has performed
in the forest Theseus nevertheless accepts in Athens. Shakespeare's
play has enabled its audience, as Oberon's play enabled the lovers,
to experience and at some level of consciousness to come to terms
with the potentially destructive and irrational as well as the creative and imaginative in themselves. Yet the success of that experience is marked by a denial of its value. Theseus scoffs at fairy
toys, and the lovers dismiss their forest drama as mere dream,
thereby allowing themselves the gratification of feeling that "the
will of man is by his reason swayed" (2.2.115). But theirs has been

be merely a bad quarto) then his omission of that play's concluding section,
in which Sly emerges from the play anxious to apply its lessons to his own
shrewish wife, suggests that he wanted to avoid didactic drama. Instead of an
audience-surrogate departing with his neat lesson in counter-uxoriousness
Shakespeare leaves his Sly in the dramatic dream, absorbed by illusions, forever unable to reemerge into the real world and his quotidian identity. But
A Midsummer Night's Dream would seem to represent an advance on this aspect of *The Shrew* in that the dramatist now assumes responsibility not only
for involving his audience but also for releasing it again. In *The Taming of
the Shrew* the audience is sacrificed to the play; in *A Midsummer Night's
Dream* the play is sacrificed to the audience, yet does its work in the very
process of being sacrificed.

a dreaming drama or a dramatic dream in which certain truths have been exposed, certain impulses released; and its benefits pass out of drama and dream into the "real" world of Athens that denies its relevance. The final graciousness of the dramatist Oberon is to sacrifice his own play for the sake of those on whom it has bestowed its blessing. Thus when he has brought all the lovers into a charmed sleep he creates for them one final illusion:

> When they next wake, all this derision
> Shall seem a dream and fruitless vision.
>
> (3.2.370–371)

Shakespeare too recognizes with amused and probably wry irony that it is the nature of a sacrificial object to be sacrificed; only then does it complete its mysterious work. In the communion of art, as in the Mass, the god is no good to the celebrant alive; he must be killed and eaten in order truly to live. But since reason must be served, as Theseus would demand, the celebrant who eats the god must, even as divinity begins to pulse within him, turn smiling away, knowing in brain if not in bloodstream that the wine was "only" wine and the bread "only" bread.

I am reminded here of Robert Penn Warren's wonderful metaphor at the opening of his article on "Pure and Impure Poetry" in which he concedes that the poem, like the monster Orillo in Boiardo's *Orlando Inamorato*, cannot be conquered piecemeal. "There is only one way to conquer the [poetic] monster: you must eat it, bones, blood, skin, pelt, and gristle. And even then the monster is not dead, for it lives in you, is assimilated into you, and you are different, and somewhat monstrous yourself, for having eaten it." [22] My metaphor of communion suggests that we absorb a kind of divinity from the poem; but in all modesty we might settle for a midpoint between gods and monsters—say, mere kingship, as implied by Eliseo Vivas's apt and eloquent statement on the same theme: "After the successful aesthetic experience the lingering memory of the object of art—the more or less clearly remembered cadenced

22 Robert Penn Warren, "Pure and Impure Poetry," in *Selected Essays of Robert Penn Warren* (New York, 1943).

lines of the poem, or the snatch of melody and the world of harmony it teasingly suggests, or the ordered world of color and space of the picture — this is carried into the mongrel world of actual men, the world of half-truth and half-justice and half-dignity. It enters it with royal authority and reorganizes it for us. It brightens it and authenticates it by serving us as the forms of the apprehension. And thus it redeems our effort." [23] In *A Midsummer Night's Dream* Shakespeare regards this "lingering memory" as very shadowy indeed, a memory that perhaps works most when least we know it. And though the aesthetic experience may exercise "royal authority" in the ordinary world, his whole play suggests that it does not enter that world with pomp and pageantry but rather with something of the cunning folksiness of a King Harry the night before Agincourt. Or with the gamesomeness of Oberon's tripping fairies; for the final image of the assimilation of art to reality and of imagination to reason is that of the fairies moving through the manor house or among the theater audience sprinkling the fictional field dew of their blessing while Puck offers to the audience the play itself, to dissolve, as the lovers did their experience, into a vision "no more yielding but a dream."

23   Eliseo Vivas, *Creation and Discovery* (Chicago: Gateway Edition, 1965), p. xxi.

VI

Richard II

THE FALL OF SPEECH

IN *Romeo and Juliet* Shakespeare's search for a genuine poetic language, one that would bind the poet to society without prostituting his art, is only partly successful. From the noise of public speech the lovers retreat to a purer style that enables the marriage of true minds but that leads inevitably to the silence of the tomb. Thus a bond between the lovers and Verona is finally forged but not while they are alive and not by means of language; it must be figured posthumously in the gold statues that memorialize the unknown private love to a wondering public.

Though of course radically different on the whole, Romeo and Juliet's self-enclosed verbal world is analogous to that which the scholars of Navarre created at the opening of *Love's Labour's Lost.* In the comedy the forbidden outside speech of the French ladies forces the locks of the scholars' verbal retreat, and the result is, if not a liberation of language, a "loosing" of speech as words acquire promiscuous license. By the end the scholars have not achieved the chiseled, death-defying fame which their monastic worship of the word was to have accorded them. But they are granted a chance at a kind of temporal fulfillment which though more vulnerable than gravestone inscriptions is also more in keeping with human nature and durable enough, if backed by constant feeling, to be called a "world-without-end bargain." Not to find the language of eternal fame — the "powerful rhyme" of Sonnet 55 that will outlive marble and the "gilded monuments Of princes" — but to learn to say "the perfect ceremony of love's rite," as Sonnet 23 puts it, is the task to which the poet should address himself.

In *Romeo and Juliet* Shakespeare learns the words of love's rite, the style that binds the lovers to each other. But like that of Navarre's scholars this style is founded on linguistic withdrawal; it binds the lovers to one another but also to death, not to Verona. At this point Shakespeare appears to sense that the poet must shape a living speech. He must find a language more durable than mere breath and yet one whose proper medium of expression is not engraved monuments but human voices. Perhaps the model he is striving to envision is Orpheus — not Orpheus the lyric poet (*Titus Andronicus* did away with him) but the Orpheus in whose dead mouth words continue to live and sing. For Shakespeare as a dramatic poet must sing *to* someone. His singing space is not the enclosed garden of the lyric poet — a prefigurement of the tomb if we believe *Romeo and Juliet* — but the stage where he engages in the most public of verbal arts and where if his speech is right it will sing in the mouths of actors long after his own is stopped.

In *A Midsummer Night's Dream* Shakespeare seems to dominate these problems. Language no longer seems a major issue; various styles are created and married with the utmost ease. It is in fact a marrying play, one in which the confirmation of private love within the Athenian temple, the multiple marriages, is metadramatically mirrored by the wedding of the play itself to its audience. But *Richard II* is a divorcing play, and one of the things it divorces is the poet from his language. In its preoccupation with the truth of language *Richard II* seems to pursue the linguistic problem that *Romeo and Juliet* raised and then quietly set aside. It is also a play that marks, I think, a decisive end to a phase of Shakespeare's artistic development, an end that presupposes a new series of beginnings conducted with linguistic equipment on which all warranties have expired.

In choosing to dramatize the fall of King Richard II Shakespeare obviates the linguistic tendency so evident in *Love's Labour's Lost* and *Romeo and Juliet* to retreat from the infectiousness of public speech and construct a private verbal sanctuary where purity is guaranteed. So long as he functions in his office the king like the playwright speaks a public tongue. His language not only binds him to society but ideally binds society, otherwise merely an aggregation of special interest groups, to itself. In this sense if the poet envies the priest who says the "perfect ceremony of love's rite," how much more must he envy the king in whose words a nation's troth is plighted, the man who can lay claim to "the King's English." Whoever claims the English crown, at any rate, claims not only England but English too, and that is a piece of property in which the poet cannot fail to have a stake. Richard the king is always prepared to usurp thrones in the kingdom of art — to play lyric poet or dramatist, elegist of self, to play the player, to direct the *de casibus* tragedy of his own deposition. But if Richard is in a sense after Shakespeare's crown, so is Shakespeare after his. He is willing at any rate to invest the poet's language in the King's English, to explore metadramatically how the king's political experience may bear on the playwright's artistic experience.[1]

Let me begin with a stylistic matter, drawing on the famous garden scene of 3.4 for an instance of duplexity. Here, in a highly ceremonial encounter that reflects the general form of the play, Richard's tristful queen learns of Richard's downfall from the regal gardener. Just before they meet, the gardener delivers a speech, the horticultural equivalent to *A Mirror for Magistrates*, in which he

1   The earliest mention of the king-dramatist metaphor in *Richard II* is by Kenneth Burke, who in a footnote in *Attitudes toward History* (New York, 1937; revised edition 1959, Los Altos, Calif., p. 277) offers the basis for a metadramatic reading of the play. Confronting the new philosophy of power-knowledge, which threatened his poetic investment in prayer, Shakespeare "dignifies his stylistic problems by transferring them to the problems of a king (whose every attempt at coercing events by prayer is promptly countered by an adverse turn in the objective situation." To my knowledge Burke has never elaborated on this footnote.

assures his apprentice that Richard's advisers, caterpillars of the commonwealth, have been duly done away with:

> They are [dead]; and Bolingbroke
> Hath seized the wasteful King. O, what pity is it
> That he had not so trimmed and dressed his land
> As we this garden! We at time of year
> Do wound the bark, the skin of our fruit-trees,
> Lest, being over-proud in sap and blood,
> With too much riches it confound itself.
> Had he done so to great and growing men,
> They might have lived to bear and he to taste
> Their fruits of duty. Superfluous branches
> We lop away, that bearing boughs may live;
> Had he done so, himself had borne the crown,
> Which waste of idle hours hath quite thrown down.
>
> (3.4.54–66)

Far from being the private sanctuary of *Romeo and Juliet* this garden is a microcosm of the entire state — England writ small — and Richard's failures have consequences ranging far beyond himself. His principal failure according to the gardener is in not exercising the proper art of cutting back, pruning, lopping away, and weeding out that prevents excesses from choking off growth and fertility. Politically the gardener's prolonged analogy sets the undisciplined and presumably undisciplining Richard in prejudicial contrast to the provident Bolingbroke. Stylistically [2] it expresses the

---

2 This rather clumsy jump from politics to stylistics is not wholly gratuitous since the very weakness of the political claims here invite us to wonder what Shakespeare is up to. That is, the gardener's argument that Richard's fall results from his failure to discipline "great and growing men" would not very much impress the former Duke of Gloucester, whom Richard disciplined straight into his grave — or for that matter Bolingbroke and Mowbray, contemplating state affairs from afar. But the gardener may be referring to Bushy, Bagot, and Green, the weedy flatterers who have grown parasitically powerful under Richard's protection. This works well in terms of Bolingbroke's contrasting treatment, his "dispatching" of Bushy and Green in 3.1. But what makes the gardener's argument unconvincing is that we have had no *dramatic* evidence, nothing staged, to indicate that Richard fails and falls as a king because he has not kept his retinue in line. (In fact there is some evidence, especially in 3.3 with Aumerle, that he falls because his retinue cannot keep *him* in line.) What we *have* seen, what we have just come from, is a confrontation in 3.3 between Richard and Bolingbroke that raises just the kind of stylistic issues to which the rest of this chapter is addressed.

problem of the poet turned dramatist that Shakespeare has worked at since *Titus Andronicus*, the problem to which T. S. Eliot applies a different metaphor when he says that "the self-education of a poet trying to write for the theatre seems to require a long period of disciplining his poetry, and putting it, so to speak, on a very thin diet." [3] The same metaphor came appropriately to Shakespeare's mind when he realized that in *Love's Labour's Lost* he had dished up "a great feast of languages" with a calorie count much too high for the rigors of dramatic action. No one has accused him of keeping the poetry of *Richard II* on a starvation diet either, especially that of Richard himself, who (to negotiate between the two "figures") cannot keep his garden of words within the belt of rule. Thus the promiscuous language of Navarre after the breakdown of Academe has its correlative in the promiscuous growth of England's garden in *Richard II*. The corrective for both would appear to be a kind of poetic restraint that enables a vigorous and fertile marriage between word and act.

As I read it then the imagery of the garden scene suggests that both poet-dramatist and poet-king need to discipline their speech to the requirements of stage and state, one of which is incisive action. At first glance Shakespeare's stylistic and England's political solution seems suggested in Bolingbroke, surely a masterful pruner and cutter-back. "My Lord Northumberland," he says indicating the hapless Bushy and Green, whose names have an almost embarrassing imagistic rightness, "see them dispatched" (3.1.35). Here, in a scene that Shakespeare has trimmed to forty-odd lines, is clipped speech with a vengeance; and this regal dispatch is obviously designed to contrast with Richard's ditherings in the following scene (3.2) where he is more inclined to tell sad stories of the deaths of kings than rouse himself to actions that might preserve a little life in one king. That Richard is infatuated with words, that his ear

> is stopped with other flattering sounds,
> As praises, of whose taste the wise are found,

3 T. S. Eliot, *Poetry and Drama* (Cambridge, Mass., 1951), p. 40.

Lascivious metres, to whose venom sound
The open ear of youth doth always listen

(2.1.17–20)

needs no documentation by this time (though it is a matter that needs returning to later). Nor does Bolingbroke's taciturnity, which has left his inner life and motives so undisclosed that equally apodictic arguments have been made for viewing him as a conniving Machiavel lusting for a crown and as a tongue-tied innocent hounded onto the throne. Everyone remembers the scenes at Flint Castle and at Westminster (3.3.186ff and 4.1.162ff) in which the man of few words stolidly insists on pushing affairs forward despite Richard's articulate lagging.

In short Shakespeare has fashioned *Richard II* much as he did *Romeo and Juliet*, in which the inertia of the lovers in their devotion to a lyric stasis is repeatedly overcome by the dramatic thrust of action occasioned by the demands of the outside world.[4] Considered in this light *Richard II* dramatizes a transfer of power from words to deeds, from a heavily ornamented, richly stylized language suited to poetic recitation to a highly functional language geared to dramatic action. In so doing the play marks a point of stylistic transition in Shakespeare's career. Richard himself points backward to the poems and sonnets, to *Romeo and Juliet*, to the word-dominated comedies *Love's Labour's Lost* and *Two Gentlemen of Verona*, and to all the high astounding speech and ponderous ceremony of the first historical tetralogy; and Bolingbroke glances stylistically forward to *Henry IV*, the mature comedies, and the tragedies.

This is all rather neat but not for that reason necessarily false unless we assume, as I think no one is likely to do, that such a stylistic transition could occur quite within one play, as though no dramatically functional speech were to be found before *Richard II* and no repetitive, lushly poetic speech after it. The search for an authentic style and a true language occupies Shakespeare throughout his literary life. We have seen one fairly explicit phase of it in

4 See the chapter on *Romeo and Juliet*, section V.

his attempt to kill off the old Petrarchan Romeo and resurrect him in purified form, rebaptized at the stylistic font of Juliet's garden. In killing off Richard in this play Shakespeare is again in some degree sacrificing the lyric poet in himself to the gods of the theater which reflect another part of himself. This is also a modification of the sacrifice depicted in *Titus Andronicus*, with Richard playing Lavinia to Bolingbroke's Goth brothers.[5] However, the revulsion present in the earlier play is now gone. The mutilation of lyric poetry by the demands of the theater for sensational action has been converted from a wild and repellent spectacle into a deposition whose stately inevitability is sanctioned by history.

As these parallels suggest, the lyric poet in Shakespeare's drama is a long time dying, not merely because he possesses the endurance of most bad habits but because he and the conceptions of language he represents have a rightful place in that drama. Bolingbroke after all is a usurper, and though his usurpation may be inevitable it is by no means fortunate. Or, to return to the garden imagery from which all this wild growth of speculation has sprung, Richard is not entirely the criminally wasteful gardener and Bolingbroke his green-thumbed successor. "Hold thy peace," the actual gardener directs his apprentice, who has been complaining of Richard's malpractice:

> He that hath suffered this disordered spring
> Hath now himself met with the fall of leaf.
> The weeds which his broad-spreading leaves did shelter,
> That seemed in eating him to hold him up,
> Are plucked up root and all by Bolingbroke,
> I mean the Earl of Wiltshire, Bushy, Green.
>
> (3.4.48–53)

Figured as the royal oak in whose protective shade rankness has parasitically fed, Richard though neglectful has a natural title to

5 Richard gains and Bolingbroke no doubt suffers too much from this comparison, but as Richard painfully learns in this play it is the nature of comparisons not to be equations. In fact if it brings one up a bit short to think of viewing *Richard II* in relation to *Titus Andronicus* that only confirms how far Shakespeare has come in so short a time; given the similarity, it is the differences that count.

the garden to which Bolingbroke — cast as an alien, intrusive autumn that defoliates the arborial Richard (and as we know ultimately uproots him no less than the weeds he has nurtured) — can make only plundering claims. If we trust the imagery, the transition from Richard to Bolingbroke is not entirely meliorative.

III

Let me turn from the stylistic issue to consider the king-as-dramatist in terms of the truth and validity of his language. On what authority, the poet may well wonder, does he utter his words? If he utters them in the old sense of "sells," he is not concerned about the authority of his words, only about a license to traffic in them — let the buyer beware, all that glitters, etc. Probably there was something of the climbing bourgeois in Shakespeare; one thinks of the coat of arms, his dealings in land, his being both sharer in his acting company and housekeeper of the Globe, his purchase of the house in Blackfriars evidently as an investment, his settling in at New Place, and so on. But it is a good deal more than probable that his hopes for his art transcended commercialism. In the sonnets art has the power to confer immortality on its subject; in *Hamlet* dramatic illusion becomes a route to truth after truth itself has turned illusive; in *King Lear* the artist-actor Edgar relies on a lyric evocation of the heights of Dover to translate Gloucester into an actor in a brief drama of spiritual redemption; in *The Winter's Tale* art gives birth to reality as Hermione materializes from the statue; and in *The Tempest* Prospero's art restores each man to himself "when no man was his own."

But still, granted that he aspires to be more than a vendor of words or a licensed liar, that he wants to claim a certain truth, meaning or order for his art, on what does the poet rely? One perfectly logical place for the young Renaissance poet to turn, as I noted with respect to *Titus Andronicus*, is to classical authorities. Plautus (*The Comedy of Errors*), Ovid (*Venus and Adonis*), Seneca (*Richard III*, *Titus Andronicus*), with perhaps some Terentian five-act structure: countersigners such as these ought to lend a certain solvency to one's art. However, as *Titus Andronicus* implies, relying on classical authorities may well render the dramatist tongue-tied as he fumbles to coordinate Ovidian language with Senecan action to suit the tastes of pit and gallery. Perhaps then, so my argument runs, Shakespeare recoils from outside authorities and in *Love's Labour's Lost* relies only on himself, seeking by sleight of dazzling speech to catch the fancy of the audience and amaze indeed the very faculty of eyes and ears. But it doesn't take him long to sense that such tactics make art's labor lost no less than love's. To stand wind and weather the poet's words must be grounded in more than his own fertile ingenuity — "Such short-lived wits do wither as they grow" — for the body he invests his words with in *Love's Labour's Lost*, though seeming solid, cannot hold out against time, death, and Mercade, the dissolver of the revels. In *Romeo and Juliet* on the other hand the lover's marriage vows are shored up by the authority of private and constant feeling (an authority in whose virtues the frustrated scholars of Navarre were to train themselves during their year-long preparation for marriage after the close of *Love's Labour's Lost*). Sequestered from the world, however, the language of Romeo and Juliet is affianced to an indwelling lyricism that the dramatic poet must gradually forgo and that we see him forgoing in *Richard II*.

When the playwright addresses himself to historical subjects he would seem to have resolved much of the difficulty since the warrant for his speech, its truth, now consists in its correspondence to the events of England's past. From this standpoint the Bastard Faulconbridge's trumpet call of patriotism at the end of *King John* — "If England to itself do rest but true" etc. — would appear to summon the dramatist to a true rendering of English history. If so it is a somewhat ironic summons in view of the fact that the summoner himself derives not from English history but from a third-rate chronicle play called *The Troublesome Raigne of John*, a play whose distortions and inventions of "history" Shakespeare made no effort to correct and whose general coherence he even addled somewhat.[6] Truth to history then seems a matter of Shakespearean

6 By cutting various scenes in *The Troublesome Raigne* that clarified events — e.g. the scene in which Faulconbridge ransacks the monastery, that in

unconcern in *King John*. That may be because history itself is so elusive. Consider for instance the death of the Duke of Gloucester about which in the opening scene of *Richard II* charges, counter-charges, and conflicting accounts whirl foggily. So foggily in fact that this scene almost appears fashioned to illustrate the unavailability of historical facts, which no doubt *ought* to come to us with all that compelling existential integrity and determinate particularity—what Alcibiades did or had done to him—that Aristotle speaks of in chapter nine of *The Poetics* but which actually come to us and to Richard's court through the mediation of symbol, style, and ceremony, retailed even in the best of cases through the distorting accounts of men imprisoned in partial perspectives.

Actually as we discover later — 1.2.4–5, 37–41; 2.1.128–131; 2.2.100–104 — it is not that history is wholly indeterminate, since everyone knows at least in a general way about Richard's complicity in the murder of Gloucester, but that it is sometimes inexpressible, for no one can accuse the Lord's anointed. No one can accuse him openly anyhow, though by indirect and crooked ways Bolingbroke directs an accusation that passes by Mowbray to find out Richard, as when he declares that Gloucester's blood "like sacrificing Abel's" cries out to him for personal revenge (1.1.104) — the quoted phrase insinuating Richard into the role of kinsman-killing Cain — which draws from Richard a rueful half-aside, "How high a pitch his resolution soars!" [7]

which the Swinstead Abbey monk discloses his plan to poison John, that in which the poisoning occurs, etc. I should add though that an increasing number of critics and editors have adopted the view first put forward by Peter Alexander in *Shakespeare's Life and Art*, London, 1938) that *The Troublesome Raigne* is a bad quarto of Shakespeare's play instead of its source, in which case the Bastard derives not from a third-rate chronicle play as I have just said but from a first-rate Shakespearean imagination operating on the random mention of a bastard in Hall's and Holinshed's chronicles. In "The Sources of *King John*," pp. 153–163 of his Signet Classics edition of the play (New York, 1966), William H. Matchett argues persuasively that Shakespeare's play, based mainly on Holinshed, preceded *The Troublesome Raigne*. In any event my point here is merely that the Bastard's forceful presence in the play testifies to Shakespeare's indifference to historical fact.

7 Richard is not without indirect and crooked verbal ways himself; thus he picks up Bolingbroke's image of flight a bit further on when, pretending to impartiality in the proceedings, he speaks of the "unstooping firmness of my

Shakespeare has so shaped this ceremonious dispute that from our perspective the truth of recent history, especially the death of Gloucester, is impossible to discover. What the dispute cries out for is a verbal authority, a fully invested guarantor of truth and justice, in short a king. But this is a play, as it is now announcing itself, about the collapse of the kind of kingly authority represented by Richard, and in this collapse he fully participates, for if the king as the spiritual and political source of truth is corrupt truth itself must disappear from high places. What we cannot realize on a first reading or viewing — the second scene with its incrimination of Richard forces a complete double take on us — is how much the apparent search for truth in the opening scene is a begged question quite subdued to the hypocrisies of a ceremonial style controlled by Richard as royal dramatist.

Richard cannot begin the play without assuring himself that the principal actors will take their proper roles and con their lines, especially Bolingbroke, of whom he asks Gaunt:

> Tell me, moreover, hast thou sounded him
> If he appeal the Duke on ancient malice,
> Or worthily, as a good subject should,
> On some known ground of treachery in him?
>
> (1.1.8–11)

Assured by Gaunt that the illusion will be maintained, that Bolingbroke's accusations will not soar to regal altitudes but remain those of "a good subject," Richard takes his seat and looks forward with anticipatory relish to the play of speech and gesture:

> Then call them to our presence. Face to face,
> And frowning brow to brow, ourselves will hear
> The accuser and the accused freely speak.
>
> (1.1.15–17)

upright soul" (1.1.121). The ambiguity is amusing. On the one hand His Royal Highness will not "stoop" to favor his relative Bolingbroke, who after all is merely a subject. On the other hand were he as the royal eagle to "stoop" on Bolingbroke, as he did on Gloucester, his cousin might not enjoy being so favored. One would expect the implications to put a notable pause in Bolingbroke's flight.

Free speech, however, which is mentioned twice again in the scene (1.1.55, 123), is precisely what Richard cannot allow; that is, "free speech" appears to mean words that go freely to the truth, but for the antagonists it actually means an unlimited volume of words. Neither Bolingbroke nor Mowbray proves short of breath in this regard, but "breath" is just what words freed from truth become, no matter how liberally given out.

How much Bolingbroke's and Mowbray's consciousness of playing roles in which true words are denied contributes to the attitude toward language implicit in their behavior, it is hard to know. However, there is much play on the subject of true speech and good words and hence on oaths and bonds. Gaunt "according to [his] oath and bond" has fetched Bolingbroke before Richard "to make good the boisterous late appeal" brought against Mowbray (1.1.2, 4). Bolingbroke, drawing himself up to the height of disputatious rhetoric — "First, heaven be the record of my speech" (1.1.30) — calls on his "body" (37), his "right drawn sword" (46), and finally his "life" (87) to reinforce his words. Mowbray's scabbard is by no means empty either, and he is as quick as Bolingbroke to get his body behind his brave. "Making good," "proving," and "maintaining" the word are terms that echo throughout the scene. Although each of the disputants has an armory well stocked with oaths, accusations, and appeals, neither of them puts his trust in speech. As Mowbray says,

> 'Tis not the trial of a woman's war,
> The bitter clamour of two eager tongues,
> Can arbitrate this cause betwixt us twain;
> The blood is hot that must be cooled for this.
>
> (1.1.48–51)

Their search for things to swear by as well as their attempts to turn words into weapons (stuffing names down each other's throat, etc.) indicates an implicit distrust of language, which is so much idle breath without the hewed flesh and congealing blood that might give it substance.

Even at this point before the play has set Richard and Bolingbroke in clear opposition, and at a time when Bolingbroke is himself given to the sweeping phrase, a fundamental gulf appears between their conceptions of language. Assuming broadly that language may serve the interests of beauty, power, and truth, it is only with the first two that Richard is concerned in this scene. We noted the aesthetic pleasure he takes in the verbal confrontation, the ritual play of speech he has arranged. But as dramatist-king he discovers, as all dramatists no doubt do, that his control over the play is far from absolute and his pleasure therefore less than complete. The players cannot keep counsel, as Hamlet says; at least they will not stick to their parts. Despite Gaunt's coaching, Bolingbroke does make a slight assay at truth, so that Richard somewhat like Claudius senses an ominous tendency of the play to disintegrate into reality. Beauty begins to give way to truth, and with truth of course Richard wants very little to do. Precisely when the authorized speech of the king should penetrate the haze of claim and counterclaim and focus illuminatively on truth Richard reneges, as indeed he must unless he wishes to incriminate himself. Truth gives way to power, or an attempt at power, as Richard commands the belligerents to pick up their gages. But no one will let him play the role of *rex ex machina* flourishing the royal word and dissolving the enmities of history into the social accord of comedy, and so he does what he does best, yields:

> We were not born to sue, but to command;
> Which, since we cannot do to make you friends,
> Be ready, as your lives shall answer it,
> At Coventry, upon Saint Lambert's day.
> . . . .
> Since we cannot atone you, we shall see
> Justice design the victor's chivalry.
>
> (1.1.196–203)

The king's power to create a political communion, to "atone" his subjects, is dependent on men's faith in his speech as an agency of truth and in him as God's authorized spokesman. With that authority spiritually if not legally in doubt, truth and justice must be sought directly from God, as Gaunt helplessly reminds the Duchess of Gloucester in the next scene:

> God's is the quarrel; for God's substitute,
> His deputy anointed in His sight,
> Hath caused [Gloucester's] death; the which if wrongfully,
> Let Heaven revenge; for I may never lift
> An angry arm against His minister.
> DUCHESS. Where then, alas, may I complain myself?
> GAUNT. To God, the widow's champion and defence.
>
> (1.2.37–43)

Thus the ordeal by words in the opening scene is transposed into the ordeal by combat in the third scene. Truth will now manifest itself in pure action unmediated by language, a deadly dumb show in which God will serve both as audience and as invisible third actor influencing the outcome. That, however, Richard cannot permit since a divine judgment against Mowbray would presumably constitute an indictment of himself as well. As earlier the play of speech could not be happily resolved, so the knightly play of arms must be aborted. As royal dramatist Richard specializes in modes of both verbal and actional incompletion; and separating the two scenes in which this is illustrated (1.1 and 1.3) is a scene whose major purpose is to illuminate Richard's moral bankruptcy as divine vicegerent.

IV

Let me gather some threads before going on. Richard and Bolingbroke stand at opposite stylistic extremes, and the transfer of political power from one to the other reflects a stylistic development Shakespeare has been working out over the course of several plays. Moreover, as the opening scene indicates, the two men hold fundamentally opposed conceptions of language. Richard's is essentially medieval, sacramental, and poetic whereas Bolingbroke's is modern, utilitarian, and scientific. In both men we see a descent from a linguistic and kingly ideal that may once have been possible (and that Richard still feels himself fulfilling) but that even in the opening scene exists merely as an empty form. This ideal is often figured in the play as Christ. It is Christ against whom Richard is repeatedly measured — sometimes unfortunately by Richard himself — and to whose burial place Bolingbroke vows to pilgrimage as the play ends. Before considering the linguistic issue in a larger theoretical context I need to look at a few instances in which Richard is unhappily compared to Christ.

The general basis for the comparison (which I shall touch on more particularly at the end of this section) lies in Richard's divine-right notion of kingship according to which he like Christ radiates divine authority in human form. As a lesser Logos Richard ought to incorporate into his political role an imitation of Christ. The first indication of his incapacity in this respect has already been alluded to: his failure to provide a political, temporal, enchoric version of the Atonement by reconciling Bolingbroke and Mowbray ("Since we cannot atone you" etc.). Born to atone his subjects, to marry with the King's English the competing factions of a territory into a nation, Richard can only divide them through banishment. Instead of the creative, redemptive speech of Christ, Richard commands only the uncreating word:

> RICHARD. Why, uncle, thou hast many years to live.
> GAUNT. But not a minute, King, that thou canst give.
> Shorten my days thou canst with sullen sorrow,
> And pluck nights from me, but not lend a morrow.
> Thou canst help Time to furrow me with age,
> But stop no wrinkle in his pilgrimage.
> Thy word is current with him for my death,
> But dead, thy kingdom cannot buy my breath.
>
> (1.3.225–232)

Confronted by a breathless Gaunt the royal word itself becomes but breath. Of course no one expects Richard's word to have Christ's power to "buy [Gaunt's] breath" when he is dead; but the rebuke reminds us that even this side of the grave Richard's words, however "current," have looked less like authentic coin of the realm than like unredeemable scrip.

This metaphor setting Christ and Richard in monetary opposition recurs most pointedly in Gaunt's famous sceptred isle speech

(2.1.40ff). An ideal England is symbolized by its "renown," gained from "Christian service and true chivalry," which rivals the renown of "the sepulchre in stubborn Jewry, / Of the world's ransom, blessed Mary's Son." And in contrast to this England of the past is that presently ruled by Richard:

> This land of such dear souls, this dear dear land,
> Dear for her reputation through the world,
> Is now leased out, I die pronouncing it,
> Like to a tenement or pelting farm.

Christ the spiritual purchaser, the "world's ransom" who in the medieval phrase "boght us with his blood agayn," has given way to Richard the self-interested, materialistic lessor of England; and as part of that descent the word "dear" shifts meaning from cherished to mere monetary value. Gaunt sharpens the issue further on saying:

> Landlord of England art thou now, not king
> Thy state of law is bondslave to the law.
>
> (2.1.113–114)

England has not been bestowed on Richard fee simple, a gift outright, but is an entailed estate which he holds in trust, the ultimate title resting with God. In signing "rotten parchment bonds" with worldly lessees Richard forfeits his bond to God. His title to kingship is now "bondslave to the law," and he who ought to be the source of law is reduced to a legal subservience that puts him on an equal footing with his subjects.[8]

---

8 In this connection W. H. Auden makes some excellent distinctions — in *The Dyer's Hand* (New York, 1962), p. 220 — between a feudal landowning economy and Renaissance mercantilism. Feudal societies, he points out, are bound together by the vow of lifelong allegiance between vassal and liege lord, whereas in a mercantile society that vow is replaced by the business contract which binds its signatories to fulfill certain specific promises by a certain date, after which their obligations to each other cease. This distinction clarifies Richard's undermining of his sacramental status, partly dependent on his ownership of land, by entering into legal contracts of limited duration, thus descending beneath the law. As Richard becomes "bankrupt, like a broken man" (2.1.257) and seizes on Bolingbroke's inheritance, Bolingbroke returns to "redeem from broking pawn the blemished crown" (2.1.293). But this kind of redemption resembles Christ's less than it does a speculative com-

Finally in the deposition scene Richard likens his experience to that of Christ: "but He, in twelve,/ Found truth in all but one; I in twelve thousand, none" (4.1.170–171). Unfortunately instead of dignifying Richard as he surely intends it to do the association forces him to suffer an impossible comparison, as Gaunt has been busily suggesting all along. The comparison is more relevant if instead of focusing on the embarrassing unlikeness of character and conduct it turns on the notion of symbolic incarnation, of Richard the man who is also God's substitute. As such Richard should ideally be neither a clear window through which men see God nor a tapestry to which the gaze is drawn for its own mortal sake but rather like a stained-glass window whose pattern is arresting in itself and yet translucently radiant with divine influence. Or to retain Gaunt's legal imagery, the divine-right king should be God's covenant with lesser men, the bond that unites the divine creditor to worldly debtors. Not Richard, however. Of his bonds to his subjects he is largely oblivious; of his ties to God he has no doubt. This has been frequently noted — his adolescent conviction of regal rightness, his feeling that the balm of the anointed king is actually his own perspiration.

What Richard experiences in his peculiarly un-Christlike fashion during the play is thus akin to Christ's passion, up to that point on the cross when seemingly dispossessed of divinity and reduced to an unsymbolic dying animal Christ cries out as one abandoned of God. This point in Richard's "passion" arrives during the depo-

mercial venture by which acquiring a crown enables Bolingbroke to acquire the crowns with which to pay off his fellow speculators:

> All my treasury
> Is yet but unfelt thanks, which more enriched
> Shall be your love and labour's recompense.
> (2.3.60–62)

Once Richard sells out his divine trust, kingship descends to merely worldly status becoming the object of commercial and political exploitation. What is paramount now is not who performs the acts and offices of kingship but who possesses the properties and revenues of kingship. Richard hastens his downfall by "capitalizing" on his durable properties, which might have temporarily sustained him in power despite his having abdicated his spiritual office — see Kenneth Burke on "Actus and Status" in *A Grammar of Motives and a Rhetoric of Motives* (Cleveland and New York, 1962), pp. 41–43.

sition scene (4.1) when the breath of worldly men, substantialized by numbers and weapons, blows away his pretensions to divinity. If the celebrated pathos of this scene falls short of tragedy it serves Shakespeare the better for that. A nobler, more Christlike Richard might have approached tragic stature; a weak sentimentalizing Richard helps disclose the inevitable poverty of the man divested of his symbolic role, much as a word repeated over and over again, however rich in original meaning, diminishes into mere noise, a rustle of air. The un-Christlike Richard pathetically reaching out for roles too large for him to play may get our qualified pity, but the widening chasm between symbol and symbolized invites our critical attention.

V

In the foregoing section I analyzed Richard as in effect a word, analogous on a lower plane of being to Christ the redemptive Logos. To expand on this, pushing matters toward the poet's sphere of interest, let us briefly consider Ernst Cassirer's theory of the development of language.[9] In Cassirer's view that development unfolds in three phases. First is an original "mimetic" phase still observable in savages and children (if the tautology is acceptable) in which an attempt is made by onomatopoesis and similar means to reproduce in speech the sensory impressions of objects so that the word as nearly as possible *is* the thing. Next is an "analogical" phase in which words become detached from their referents yet still resemble them. Third is a "symbolic" phase in which words lose their sensuous character entirely, becoming arbitrary signs to which abstract meanings are attached.

This view of linguistic evolution has its Elizabethan analogue in the notion of the Great Chain of Being, at the bottom of which we find in inorganic substances matter devoid of spirit and at the top, in God, spirit devoid of matter. The concept of incarnation to which such a hierarchy gives rise — the god in Jesus, the soul in the body, the divinely appointed king in the mortal man, impanation —

9 Ernst Cassirer, *Language*, vol. 1 of *The Philosophy of Symbolic Forms* (New Haven, Conn., 1953), pp. 186–198.

has also a verbal form, one that gives appropriateness to the conception of Christ as Logos, in that as a phonetic aggregation the Word is the corporeal substance into which the spirit of its symbolizing capacity is infused.

In Cassirer's mimetic phase the bond between word and thing is so close that what is done to the one is done to the other; word-magic becomes possible, which is why primitives are reluctant to disclose their true names, freshmen to sign term papers, and God to emerge from the ineffability of the tetragrammaton.[10] In Shakespeare's time a belief in word-magic still persisted as part of a more general faith in the inherent rightness of words.[11] The "curse of

10 In a more sophisticated sense I suppose we all accept the fact that what is done to the name is also done to the thing — that is, we acknowledge that although there is no phono-mimetic bridge between words and things language is nonetheless constitutive of reality, our minds reflecting not on things but on named things. Thus Kenneth Burke can say that "for man, nature is emblematic of the spirit imposed upon it by man's linguistic genius" (*Language as Symbolic Action*, Berkeley, Calif., 1966, p. 362). More specifically, in urging that names are not merely tags attached to objects but means of interpreting and shaping reality, Ernst Cassirer observes how the Greek term for moon, *mēn*, constitutes that planetary object as an instrument for measuring time whereas the Latin *luna* constitutes it as a source of illumination (*Language*, p. 173). And in a very interesting "Postscript to Chapters III and IV" in *Structural Anthropology* (New York, 1967) Claude Lévi-Strauss points out that even the phonetic features of the French *fromage* and the English *cheese* cause that species of fermented milk to materialize differently for us.

A good many modern critics and even poets, foreheads villainous low, regard this constitutive feature of language as an interfering form of mediation between "raw reality" and us. Like Juliet they assume a "What does it matter what you call it?" position, seeing too much what language does *to* poets, too little what it does *for* them — or from the standpoint of "reality" becoming overly conscious of how language obscures things (of how *mēn*, by not being *luna*, darkens the moon unduly) and insufficiently conscious of how it liberates their qualities (*mēn* after all lighting up one important feature, lunar periodicity). But no poet really adopts Juliet's position while writing his poem. Thus the direst linguistic skepticism sometimes gets expressed, by an Ionesco or a Beckett for instance, in works whose language has been most sedulously chosen and crafted, rather as poems proclaiming the utter collapse of meaning in the world manage to except themselves.

11 M. M. Mahood has a good summary of Elizabethan attitudes toward language, ranging from the skeptical to the credulous, in *Shakespeare's Wordplay* (London, 1957), pp. 168–175. I should take this chance also to record my indebtedness to her fine chapter on *Richard II* (pp. 73–88), a quasi-metadramatic treatment of the play in that Miss Mahood takes it to "be about the efficacy of a king's words" (p. 73) though she does not emphasize its self-reflective features or regard it as a watershed in Shakespeare's development.

Rome" that lighted on Henry VIII and Elizabeth or that of the Hebrews that fell on Spinoza later was phrased in such mace-and-chain terms that its victims must have inspected themselves for bruises after each period. Another more common kind of word-magic was vested in the priest, who might if Catholic transform reality or if Protestant strip from it its superficial appearances by uttering at the right time and place the phrase "This is my body, this is my blood." The king too, no less than pope and priest, could impose the shape of his speech on reality. Mowbray swears in the opening scene by the kingly sword that laid his knighthood on his shoulder (1.1.78), but it is less the king's sword than his verbal authority that enables him to transform men from commoners to knights, from knights to dukes, almost literally to "make" men. For like pope and priest the king inherits from God a share of verbal creativity, the original "let there be and there was" aspect of speech.

Naturally the king's verbal wand must not wave too randomly. "Let there be a convening of Parliament" will no doubt produce a convened Parliament; but "Let Anne Boleyn be queen" produced no immediate evidence of linguistic magic. Nor should the king emulate the professor of philosophy at Pisa who not merely refused to look through Galileo's telescope but attempted through sheer eloquence and logical phrasing to charm those vexatious new planets out of the heavens. Yet there is much of the Pisan professor in Richard, especially on his return from Ireland:

> Is not the King's name twenty thousand names?
> Arm, arm, my name! a puny subject strikes
> At thy great glory. (3.2.85–87)

The Pisan professor probably felt that he could call planets from the vasty skies on the authority of Aristotle. Richard's authority, the high source of the glory refulgent in his name and speech, is of course God; and more than any other Shakespearean king he assumes the operation of a medieval concept of world order and a divine-right notion of kingship. Careful study of Tillyard's *The Elizabethan World Picture* has taught him that meaning is created by God and stands at the bidding of the king. That means that his task is not so much to generate order as to imitate and maintain it.

Backed by God's infinite treasury the king's word is automatically good, divinely certified as a substantial entity, whereas the language of ordinary men must seem mere breath:

> The breath of worldly men cannot depose
> The deputy elected by the Lord.
> For every man that Bolingbroke hath pressed
> To lift shrewd steel against our golden crown,
> God for his Richard hath in heavenly pay
> A glorious angel. (3.2.56–61)

The words of worldly men cannot, in the secondary sense of "depose," testify against God's anointed since only his words, analogous as they are to the coin (the "angels") which he alone is authorized to mint, are legal tender.

But with Richard's authority in question the distinction between counterfeit and real coin and between breath and divinely inspired speech begins to disappear. Richard finds himself in a situation like that of the pope later on, who according to the translators of the King James Bible suffered from what is nowadays called a credibility gap:

> If [wise men] were sure that their high Priest had all laws shut up in his breast, as Paul the Second bragged, and that he were as free from error by special privilege as the Dictators of Rome were made by law inviolable, it were another matter; then his word were an Oracle, his opinion a decision. But the eyes of the world are now open, God be thanked, and have been a great while, they find that he is subject to the same affections and infirmities that others be, that his skin is penetrable, and therefore so much as he proveth, not as much as he claimeth, they grant and embrace.[12]

12 *The Translators to the Readers: Preface to the King James Version 1611*, ed. Edgar J. Goodspeed (Chicago, 1935), p. 36. Bringing in the pope's declining authority as analogy here helps suggest how richly compressed within this play are some of the large issues of the times, or of how in Eliseo Vivas's terms the "subsistent" cultural values of Shakespeare's times have been made "insistent" in *Richard II*. In the opening scene for instance — where Richard in the role of God's spokesman tries to ceremonialize the Bolingbroke-Mowbray quarrel while they, on the other hand, are anxious to bypass symbolic dealings and get straight on to the field of combat — we can easily see a version of a major Reformation issue, direct access to divine truth as opposed to institutional mediation. Or since this issue can be fitted into a general historical

As Richard puts it:

> I live with bread like you, feel want,
> Taste grief, need friends: subjected thus,
> How can you say to me I am a king?
>
> (3.2.175–177)

The process by which the king becomes "subjected thus," a wedge being driven between the role and the man, extends to the king's language as well. Like the pope's, his word gradually ceases to be an oracle and his opinion a decision. This divisive process traced by the play as a whole is also involved in the development of language from Cassirer's mimetic to his symbolic phase. The natural conjunction of word and thing — of, in the word itself, phonic substance and signification — comes apart. Prior to or behind or above this disjunctive movement stands the figure of Christ the divine Logos, the Word that *is* but also *means*, the mortal man from whose body the god will reascend. In Richard, the divine king incarnate in man, the resurrection is inverted. Role and man disengage, and Richard no longer signifies but merely is, an amorphous undefined nothing, the human equivalent to the mere breath to which his once substantial speech has dwindled:

> I have no name, no title;
> No, not that name was given me at the font,
> But 'tis usurped. Alack the heavy day,
> That I have worn so many winters out
> And know not now what name to call myself!
>
> (4.1.255–259)

movement away from symbolic systems (actually only a substitution of newer symbolic systems for older ones), we might move from religion to science and associate Mowbray and Bolingbroke with empiricism. Like Bacon and Hobbes and the Royal Academy they prefer their reality undoctored by language. Just as Bacon's conception of "dialogue" was two people observing the same laboratory experiment, so Bolingbroke and Mowbray locate truth not in speech but in silent deeds. I am not suggesting that *Richard II* is a complex allegory about the decline of the papacy and the rise of Protestantism and empirical science. But in its own symbolic structure, deeply enchased, the play contains with a richness and clarity not given to Hooker or Bacon or Descartes or Locke the values implicit in a vast movement of culture from the medieval toward the modern.

It is the same fate he dealt to Bolingbroke when he deprived him of lands and title. York had predicted all:

> Take Hereford's rights away, and take from Time
> His charters and his customary rights;
> Let not tomorrow then ensue today;
> Be not thyself; for how art thou a king
> But by fair sequence and succession?
>
> (2.1.195–199)

In a Renaissance-medieval world order based on analogy, to disinherit Hereford is to disinherit oneself. The process begins in earnest when Bolingbroke returns to England, a meaning seeking a name that can express his substance to the world:

> BERKELEY. My Lord of Hereford, my message is to you.
> BOLINGBROKE. My Lord, my answer is — to Lancaster;
> And I am come to seek that name in England;
> And I must find that title in your tongue,
> Before I make reply to aught you say. (2.3.69–73)

As verbal power in the play transfers from Richard to Bolingbroke the grounds of its authority change. From the opening scene Bolingbroke has regarded words as vocal conveniences whose substance resides in what they designate. Unlike Richard he has never accepted the bond between word and thing, the bond that enables the word to create, or as in Richard's practice to destroy, the thing. When in the deposition scene Richard flings the mirror to the floor Bolingbroke makes a typical distinction between symbols and things:

> RICHARD. Mark, silent king, the moral of this sport,
> How soon my sorrow hath destroyed my face.
> BOLINGBROKE. The shadow of your sorrow hath destroyed
> The shadow of your face. (4.1.290–293)

Their conflicting attitudes toward symbols are natural enough at this point: Richard the man being separated from his symbolic title of king insisting on the bondedness of names to things, Bolingbroke equally insistent that symbols are no more welded to things than kingly titles are to men like Richard.

If Bolingbroke returns to England as a meaning in search of a name — ultimately the name of King Henry IV — the name must of necessity be merely a label attached to the man. Moreover the meaning with which Bolingbroke would substantialize the name is less himself than material force. In the opening scene, for instance, he and Mowbray cannot let words stand alone unreinforced by action; they have blood to let and a great haste to be doing. Then on his return journey through the wilds of Gloucestershire when Northumberland says that his "fair discourse hath been as sugar" seasoning the way, Bolingbroke replies, "Of much less value is my company/ Than your good words" (2.3.6–7, 19–20). Not his own speech but the good words behind him, the votes, give him meaning. And the point is driven home forcefully at Flint Castle when Richard comes glistering down into the base court — his only weapons being verbal drafts on a divine account that has long been overdrawn — to encounter the future "silent king" whose intentions are communicated not by speech but by the blunt expressiveness of twenty thousand armed bodies.

In the deposition scene Richard the name without a meaning confronts Bolingbroke the meaning without a name. The dramatic and political issue centers not merely in who will possess the word in England but in what conception of language will prevail. With Richard's fall the possibility of a sacramental language falls too. The possibility had actually disappeared long ago, but now Richard comes to realize his loss. The King's English he had thought Richard's English as he had thought the land of England his land, ceded outright. Both he had in reality merely held in trust, and that trust has been violated. Though his general bankruptcy has been public knowledge for some time — "The King's grown bankrupt, like a broken man" (2.1.257) — he now takes personal possession of at least that unpleasant fact:

> An if my word be sterling yet in England,
> Let it command a mirror hither straight,
> That it may show me what a face I have
> Since it is bankrupt of his majesty.
>
> (4.1.264–267)

His word remains "sterling" and the mirror is fetched only because Bolingbroke is willing to extend Richard's credit a bit further before making all his debts payable on demand, not with sovereigns but with the sovereign's life. Before Richard makes that final balloon payment, however, he must undergo at Pomfret Castle the spiritual consequences of his deposition.

VI

Losing his name Richard loses everything. Cast out of his medieval world of preestablished order and significance he is isolated in Pomfret Castle where he attempts bootlessly to create meanings that had once simply been there for his taking. What he experiences is a concrete version of the whole Renaissance and modern process by which the primordial marriage of word and thing, symbol and symbolized, was put asunder and man's thought divorced from his world. Bacon, Hobbes, Descartes, Locke, and the Royal Society are all just around the historical corner about to give discursive and philosophical expression to issues that the poet has already incarnated in drama. This large divorce is implicit in Cassirer's three-phase evolution of verbal symbolism. Mistakenly, I think, Cassirer assumes that the passage of language through these three phases involves progressive improvement. The brute stuff of mimetic sound is gradually distilled and left behind as the liberated symbolic capacity of speech runs like a Marvellian drop of dew "into the Glories of the Almighty Sun," or at least soars straight to things and ideas.

For the poet this separation of words as phonic objects from words as arbitrary symbols is hardly the melioristic process Cassirer makes it out to be. It is analogous not to a Platonic liberation of the soul from the body but to the Fall — or in political metaphor more suitable to a history play, to the deposition of a divine-right king. For if the poet could draw on a language intrinsically bound to things, still trailing clouds of the original magic with which God swathed it, then the very materials of his trade would be endowed with truth, beauty, and power. Merely through the exercise of his art the poet would put himself in daily contact with God and God's natural order, thus giving the lie to the popular Renaissance rift be-tween art and nature. A thing devoutly to be wished. But if I read *Richard II* correctly Shakespeare dramatizes in it the surrender of hope that such a language is available to the poet. Because it is a thing so devoutly to be wished he surrenders hope in it reluctantly and eloquently, giving to the Richard of the last three acts a pathos that the Richard of the first two acts by no means merits and re-peatedly capitalizing on the widespread symbolic appeal generated by such a language and the world order it implies.

For the world order, the shape of reality, sustains and is sus-tained by the language. It is an order medieval and Elizabethan, full of chains and cosmic dances, harmonies and hierarchies of being, and kings who are the suns of their societies — a rational, divinely orchestrated, eternal order that man in his finite sphere can but ad-mire and imitate. More important it is a world order that man's lan-guage imitates and that the king's sacramental language, given his authority, magically participates in. "Is not the King's name twenty thousand names?" If it were — if God's order were reflected in a language that man inherited from God's word — then word and thing, language and nature, the king's name and twenty thousand soldiers would be reciprocally defining if not identical. If it were. But alas for poet and king, it is not.

In the world of fact where Bolingbroke holds court words are no more permanently enchased in things than Richard is in the English throne. Like kings (though as an about-to-be king Boling-broke does not press the association) language is a social conven-ience whose authority derives from common consent, not from on high, and whose meanings reflect the finite time-ridden needs of men, not God's eternal cosmic order. If this does not necessarily imply that the Elizabethan world picture is just that, a picture that may be taken down and replaced by another, it at least argues that man is no longer wedded to that world order by means of speech. This realization gradually invades Richard's consciousness after his return from Ireland and takes full possession of him in Pomfret Castle. It is in Shakespeare's consciousness too, where, however, he possesses it, not the other way around, and hence can figure it forth as the poet's as well as the king's concern.

In a long note appended to *The Imperial Theme* G. Wilson Knight analyzes Richard's prison soliloquy at 5.5.1–66 as Shakespeare's commentary on the act of poetic creation.[13] His analysis, typically penetrating, suffers a bit from his not taking account of how the burden of prior action bears on the speech and imparts a particular exigency to the poet's creative plight. For the poet who has not experienced the bifurcation of world and language, who still deals confidently in mimetic speech, really has no creative plight and may in a sense be said not to create at all. His poetic task is defined in advance, not discovered in the act of creation; he must celebrate the world order by imitating it in words in which that order is already implicit. Truth, as correspondence between statement and reality, the unfallen poet need not search out but merely affirm, for to the hierarchic structure of reality corresponds a hierarchy of linguistic truths. But destroy the bond between language and nature, remove the divine sanctions from speech, and mark what verbal discord follows. Lacking an authority to distinguish higher from lower truths, words contend anarchically against words:

> For no thought is contented. The better sort,
> As thoughts of things divine, are intermixed
> With scruples and so set the word itself
> Against the word.   (5.5.11–14)

In this there is as much potential despair for the poet as for the king. Not only are his own vatic powers (dependent on his knowledge of the mysteries of words) rescinded, but his very medium is taken from him and distributed among the populace. No longer does he who has the greatest command of words have thereby the command of things too. Once language loses its inherent meaning and order these fall to the mercy of the masses or become the temporary property of anyone who, backed by the masses as Boling-

13 G. Wilson Knight, *The Imperial Theme* (London, 1931; Methuen edition, 1958), pp. 351–367.

broke is, is sufficiently powerful and unscrupulous to seize verbal authority for himself.

Divorced from the world then and compelled to work in a medium devoid of guarantees, on what can the poet rely? Perhaps we should study Richard, who says:

> I have been studying how I may compare
> This prison where I live unto the world;
> And for because the world is populous
> And here is not a creature but myself,
> I cannot do it. Yet I'll hammer it out.
> My brain I'll prove the female to my soul,
> My soul the father.
>
> (5.5.1–7)

And so on. The gulf between himself and the world he painfully acknowledges; the soliloquy issues from that fact and attempts to undo it by building a bridge of words across the gulf. This verbal sculpting is not just a mimetic reflection of an existent order but — "Yet I'll hammer it out" — an unaided generative act performed, as the prologue to Act 5 of *Henry V* puts it, "in the quick forge and working-house of thought." What Richard hammers out is one metaphor, simile, conceit, analogy after another, each reinforcing his grand design to make of his prison room an everywhere and of himself all men, the most elaborate being his association of himself with the clock so that "sighs and tears and groans/ Show minutes, times, and hours" (57–58).

Richard, however, has been long addicted to metaphor. But always before, before he became aware of the disjunction between speech and reality, his words whether metaphoric *or* literal were in his view bonded to things.

> The hopeless word of "never to return"
> Breathe I against thee, upon pain of life.
>
> (1.3.152–153)

Breathed against Mowbray such words create the condition they express, blowing Mowbray abroad as forcibly as the sea breezes. A more memorable example of the fusion of kingly speech to reality is provided by Richard's remission of part of Bolingbroke's sentence, which draws from even that skeptic an awed comment:

> How long a time lies in one little word!
> Four lagging winters and four wanton springs
> End in a word. Such is the breath of kings.
>
> (1.3.213–215)

When the world responds with such alacrity to regal breath the king must feel that his metaphors are not wholly metaphoric. So at the opening of 3.2 on his return from Ireland Richard can greet the earth "as a long-parted mother with her child" (8) and seem almost to believe it as "weeping, smiling" he caresses the ground and exhorts nature at some length to mobilize herself in his defense. The foolishness of this he can acknowledge — "Mock not my senseless conjuration, lords" (23) — but he cannot sustain for very long a disbelief in the magical efficacy or mimetic accuracy of his speech. Thus he returns immediately to the figurative mode and spins out a heroic simile that depends on the entire medieval and Elizabethan world order:

> Discomfortable cousin! know'st thou not
> That when the searching eye of heaven is hid
> Behind the globe, that lights the lower world,
> Then thieves and robbers range abroad unseen
> In murders and in outrage boldly here;
> But when from under this terrestrial ball
> He fires the proud tops of the eastern pines
> And darts his light through every guilty hole,
> Then murders, treasons, and detested sins,
> The cloak of night being plucked from off their backs,
> Stand bare and naked, trembling at themselves?
> So when this thief, this traitor, Bolingbroke,
> Who all this while hath revelled in the night
> Whilst we were wandering with the antipodes,
> Shall see us rising in our throne, the east,
> His treasons will sit blushing in his face,
> Not able to endure the sight of day,
> But, self-affrighted, tremble at his sin.
> Not all the water in the rough rude sea
> Can wash the balm off from an anointed king;

> The breath of worldly men cannot depose
> The deputy elected by the Lord. . . .   (3.2.36–57)

We are wrong, I think, if we attribute Richard's hyperbolic claims about the consubstantiality of king, sun, and God merely to his extravagance of mind and self-dramatizing tendencies. When the world order is itself infiltrated by analogy in response to its divine author whose creative and regulative impulses are metaphoric,[14] then kings and suns do not have only a curious invented resemblance but are indeed consubstantial. By the same token metaphor is not merely a verbal device with which to align symbolic counters, a means of ingeniously passing off half-truths as whole truths — it is not in short a lie, as it must be when considered in the light of empirical logic, but rather an authentic reflection of the world's true shape and nature.

So Richard believes in his metaphors (or if we like *dis*believes in them since for him they are not "metaphoric" but claims of identity) as he believes in the mimetic truth of his language generally. For him language and reality are facing each other like mirrors reflecting in mutual confirmation a single closed system.[15] As

14 This point about an analogical world order hardly needs documenting, I suppose, especially since a generation of English graduate students has by now learned to answer examination questions on any subject from Chaucer to Samuel Johnson by delivering a two-page discourse on the Great Chain of Being. However, the book of that title by Arthur O. Lovejoy should perhaps be mentioned, along with E. M. W. Tillyard's *The Elizabethan World Picture* (New York, 1944), Lily B. Campbell's *Shakespeare's Tragic Heroes* (Cambridge, 1930), Hardin Craig's *The Enchanted Glass* (New York, 1936), Theodore Spencer's *Shakespeare and the Nature of Man* (New York, 1960), Marjorie Nicolson's *The Breaking of the Circle* (rev. ed., New York, 1960), and Hiram Haydn's *The Counter-Renaissance* (New York, 1950).

15 So it seems a bit out of focus to say, as it so often is said, that Richard contents himself with symbols and ceremony in contrast to Bolingbroke, who is content only with facts, realities, deeds. It is hard not to say this occasionally since it is true; but it is more fully true to say that Richard covets symbol and ceremony not for their own sake exclusively, like a miser with money, but because he believes that they participate in facts, realities, deeds. A fine pair of articles — Joan Webber's "The Renewal of the King's Symbolic Role: From *Richard II* to *Henry V*," *Texas Studies in Literature and Language*, 4(1963):530–538, and Eric La Guardia's "Ceremony and History: The Problem of Symbol from *Richard II* to *Henry V*" in *Pacific Coast Studies in Shakespeare*, ed. Waldo F. McNeir and Thelma N. Greenfield (Eugene, Ore.,

long as Richard remains within that tautological system he is as hard to refute as Newton or Freud or Frye. However, the business of the play is to thrust him forth into exile where he may recognize that symbolic as well as actual mirrors can falsify. So in the deposition scene he hurls his mirror to the floor and with it his belief in the mimetic truth of his language. When that happens the King's world shatters too, and he knows with something of Donne's dismay that "'Tis all in peeces, all coherence gone;/ All just supply, and all Relation." [16]

Richard's self-conscious and thought-ridden hammering out of metaphors in Pomfret Castle, metaphors that are now "merely" metaphors, is thus a perfect index of his linguistic alienation from the world. More than that though. If metaphor marks his estrangement from the world it also is the means by which he attempts to return to its ambit. Metaphor is also the instrument of the poet, who has as great a stake in this as the king. In a society whose exile from nature is consequent on its devaluation of words to the status of arbitrary conveniences the poet will seek to rekindle something

1966) – keep all the issues in just balance. The lines of my own interpretation run mostly parallel to theirs, but there are enough divergences among the three for each to claim that he alone has heard the guru's voice distinctly. Another helpful article on the second tetralogy, one that deals metadramatically with the state-stage metaphor, is Leonard Dean's "From *Richard II* to *Henry V*: A Closer View," in *Studies in Honor of DeWitt T. Starnes*, ed. Thomas P. Harrison and James H. Sledd (Austin, Texas, 1967).

16 This process began well before the deposition scene, as early as 3.2 when nature begins to prove unresponsive to Richard's language and desires. "O, call back yesterday, bid time return," Salisbury cries, "And thou shalt have twelve thousand fighting men!" (3.2.69–70). And Richard in an image forecasting his dashing down of the mirror in the deposition scene begins to sense the separability of himself and the world:

> But now the blood of twenty thousand men
> Did triumph in my face, and they are fled;
> And, till so much blood thither come again,
> Have I not reason to look pale and dead?
> (3.2.76–79)

From this point on, and especially in his speech about the "hollow crown/ That rounds the mortal temples of a king" (3.2.160–170), Richard is increasingly aware of the fact that his words are merely words, his metaphors merely metaphors. His Pomfret Castle speech, however, culminates the long process and hence deserves special attention.

of the word's lost glory. That he can recover the adolescent naiveté and even arrogance of regarding language as God's personal gift to him, its words fresh from the divine mint and golden with inherent value, is past the size of dreaming. Truth, meaning, order, and value will no longer come resident in language but must be labored for in the smithy of his own mind and hammered into the insubstantial stuff of speech.[17]

So the poet's task is to restore to words a portion of their original dignity if not their original meaning. He cannot restructure words into the temples they once were, fixed dwelling places of the god, but neither can he allow them to serve merely as way stations for men's traveling and trivial meanings. What the poet *can* do is by no means self-evident. As I read them the metadramatic implications of Richard's experience are that the poet is left to construct meaning and value not by means of but *in* words, to create out of

17   One could call this the poet's version of the existentialist experience, though I am not suggesting that Shakespeare is a forerunner of existentialism, certainly not in the way Walter Kaufman does in *From Shakespeare to Existentialism* (New York, 1960) where Shakespeare is found congenial to the philosophical movement because selective quotation can make out an unchristian aspect to the plays. I mean rather that the poet, deprived of a natural language and caught up in a verbal absurd, finds his world of words decomposing like the existentialist's actual world into the merely existent, "is-ness." With the collapse of the bright surfaces of signification words become no more than a gray phonetic vapor, *flatus vocis*, which gives rise in the poet to Richard's nausea and hopelessness. At the same time, in Richard's or the fallen poet's turning to metaphor, we can discern an attempt by no means promising at this stage to re-create meaning, to channel the world's substance back into the emptied sounds. Being now of age, however, and having experienced what he has experienced, the poet knows that he enters on his task of re-creation alone, sustained by nothing more absolute than his own will to engage in the enterprise. There is no doubt arrogance in that, and courage too, but more than that, the humility of committing himself to a search for order that will serve not himself finally but his art and his language.
    In our time a further development occurs. Whereas Richard reaches out toward the world with metaphor in an attempt to restore something of its lost significance, advocates of the *nouveau roman* like Alain Robbe-Grillet simply accept the brute "thereness" of the world and quite reject the metaphors with which literature has anthropomorphically furnished it (M. Robbe-Grillet, for instance, would resent my adjective "brute"; see his *For a New Novel: Essays on Fiction*, trans. Richard Howard, New York, 1965). Thus we pass from a nature directly reflected in, to a nature only metaphorically reflected in, to a nature utterly alienated from man's language — which is roughly the movement Cassirer charts from the mimetic to the symbolic.

the unlikely drab material of sound a true eloquence, to make a world of and in a prison cell. But he must somehow do this in the clear knowledge that like the king he is uncrowned, without natural authority, and subject to time. If as a dramatist he plays "in one person many people," populating an entire stage with his own thoughts, he must know how swiftly those many people can telescope into his own person again and he be deposed from kingly creator to "nothing." For the validity of his created world — the cloud-capped towers, the gorgeous palaces, the solemn temples that assume such brave shape and solidity in the theater — is as flimsy as Richard's prison metaphors. Still if he cannot claim substantive literalness for either his metaphors or the dramatic world they unfold, neither can he permit them to dissolve into make-believe: bare prison cells unconvincingly tricked out to play at being real. For once the prison cell has gone through the poet's mind and into his language it is never quite the same again.

These are complex matters to which the play offers no final or even tentative solutions; it is enough that Shakespeare has brilliantly dramatized a dilemma of continuing urgency to him. Indeed given the nature of the dilemma — the poet's exile from verbal paradise into a fallen state where words seem hopelessly alienated from a divinely certified world order that is itself not beyond question — a final solution of any sort is impossible. The whole thrust of the play implies the poet's awareness that he now writes not within and in imitation of a world order but toward an order of his own making — or better, toward *orders* of his own making. For each play presents a new chaos of words awaiting the shaping hammer of imaginative thought, and its writing is an occasion not to reaffirm the truth of an order outside itself but to discover an order whose truth is unique to itself and certified by no authority but its own vision. In this sense the poet from this point on, as the sweet singer from Saginaw has put it, learns by going where he has to go.

VII

With Richard deposed and Bolingbroke enthroned a new order seems in the making. Given Bolingbroke's general symbolic skepticism we might expect him to institute a political order based on a maximum of manipulative efficiency and a minimum of ceremonial show. Manipulative efficiency is achieved, however, not by eschewing the panoply of ritual, ceremony, and verbal display with which Richard girded kingship but by employing it with a clear awareness that it is a means and not an end. Bolingbroke can no more dispense with the symbolic trappings of majesty and acquire direct access to truth than he can dispense with the name of king and yet achieve full political power. That, I take it, is why we encounter at the beginning of Act 4 a perfect repetition of the beginning of Act 1, a scene of ritualized contention in which words fly up and gages are thrown down but in which the real truth about Aumerle is no more available than it was about Mowbray. At first glance little seems to have changed since Richard's fall. But the difference is that Bolingbroke's plays of state are directed exclusively to an audience of men, not to God, as indeed we might have expected from the politician who has always had an actor's eye on the pit — "Off goes his bonnet to an oyster-wench" etc. (1.4.23–36). So his biggest scene must be carefully staged for "the common view":

> Fetch hither Richard, that in common view
> He may surrender; so we shall proceed
> Without suspicion.
>
> (4.1.155–157)

Although Bolingbroke has much the same difficulty Richard had (1.1) getting the actors to stick to their lines — Richard seizing the occasion to preside over his own deposition — unlike Richard he is able to force the play to a conclusion. As Richard tries to dilate verbally on the pathos of his situation Bolingbroke and Northumberland keep insisting that the plot go forward, the play be played out:

> BOLINGBROKE. I thought you had been willing to resign.
>
> (4.1.190)
>
> NORTHUMBERLAND. My lord, dispatch; read o'er these articles.
>
> (4.1.243)

For otherwise, as Northumberland says, "The commons will not then be satisfied" (4.1.272). The stress on the commons during the deposition is in keeping with the general degrading of symbolic forms as power shifts from Richard to Bolingbroke. It is Bolingbroke, "king of smiles" as Hotspur later calls him, who knows and demonstrates that political power does not descend from God but arises from the people, that words do not have intrinsic meanings but only those meanings with which men invest them, and therefore that the ritual play of state is valuable not as mimesis of divine order but as a tactical device, an edifying spectacular designed to promote political order, obedience, loyalty.[18]

Even so Bolingbroke's interest in the populace would appear to go at least partway toward remedying Richard's self-absorbed indifference and hence to suggest the possibility of a national "atonement" so lacking under the earlier regime. Such a possibility seems even nearer in 5.3 when Bolingbroke forgives the would-be traitor Aumerle. With the word set against the word, the French "pardonne moi" against the English "pardon" (see 5.3.111–135), Bolingbroke chooses the redemptive word and so registers a certain moral claim to the King's English. Unfortunately the chance of a lasting atonement quickly vanishes, literally through a slip of the tongue. Returning from Pomfret Castle with the dead Richard "all breathless," the fawning Exton discovers that his "deed of slander" will be paid by "neither [the King's] good word nor princely favour" (5.6.31, 35, 42). However, Exton's self-righteous explanation of the murder, if it does not exonerate himself, sets Bolingbroke permanently outside the pale of political and spiritual grace: "From your own mouth, my lord, did I this deed" (5.6.37). Here in the mouth of the man who has always deprecated words as

18 The point is forcefully made when in a moment of political hubris Bolingbroke prematurely announces "In God's name, I'll ascend the regal throne," thereby prompting the Bishop of Carlisle's "Marry, God forbid!" (4.1.113–114). Carlisle goes quickly on to expound the orthodox position regarding divine-right kingship, after which Northumberland says approvingly "Well have you argued, sir, and for your pains/ Of capital treason we arrest you here" (150–151). So much for divine right. Bolingbroke may not ascend the throne "in God's name," but he can ascend it in the name of an applauding populace and twenty thousand armed men.

breath is a potency of speech reminiscent of the primitive magic Richard thought his words possessed. What that implies of course is not that words are after all laden with magical efficacy. The killing force of Bolingbroke's "Have I no friend will rid me of this living fear?" derives from the fact that his words are laden with money, not manna. As Exton readily senses, there is a rustle of reward in the voice of a king who strewed his route to kingship with postdated drafts on the royal exchequer. Typically with Bolingbroke, value lies behind the word, not in it; but the promise of that value has a galvanic effect on men like Exton: "Come, let's go./ I am the King's friend, and will rid his foe" (5.4.10–11).

Neither in Richard's final soliloquy then nor in Bolingbroke's promise to pilgrimage to the Holy Land to absolve himself of guilt is there much evidence of an assured future for the poet. Both have richly contributed to the devaluation of speech. Richard, having deprived the word of moral and spiritual substance, has only the title of kingship, the name but not the thing, when he encounters Bolingbroke. To redeem the pawned crown and the King's English Bolingbroke employs words as promissory notes, filling the vacuum left in the word by the withdrawal of God with the new meaning of himself backed by political power and popular support. From Richard the name without the thing we proceed to Bolingbroke the thing without the name — the man lacking divine authority and legitimate title to kingship, the usurper who confiscates the word for his own purposes. The King's English remains bankrupt, especially when Bolingbroke loses the popular support on which his claim to kingship rested — that is in the *Henry IV* plays where Bolingbroke is portrayed as a guilt-ridden king whose land is subject to repeated broils. The redemption of the word is beyond Bolingbroke. It is a task left apparently to the man who is himself in sore need of redeeming, the young Prince Hal:

> So, when this loose behaviour I throw off
> And pay the debt I never promised,
> By how much better than my word I am,
> By so much shall I falsify men's hopes;
> And like bright metal on a sullen ground,

My reformation, glittering o'er my fault,
Shall show more goodly and attract more eyes
Than that which hath no foil to set it off.
I'll so offend, to make offence a skill,
Redeeming time when men think least I will.

(*1 Henry IV*, 1.2.231–240)

But that is well beyond my present reach and too complicated to submit to tidy summaries. Moreover as I suggested at the end of the previous section there is no permanent redemption to be had, no final order or eternal truth, but something like a series of verbal holding actions in which the poet staves off chaos now one way, now another. Or as a modern poet puts it, one who unlike Shakespeare at this point found absolutes to keep chaos at bay, even to encompass it:

And so each venture
Is a new beginning, a raid on the inarticulate
With shabby equipment always deteriorating
In the general mess of imprecision of feeling,
Undisciplined squads of emotion.

(*East Coker*)

Richard II looks nostalgically back on a time or on the possibility of a time, somewhere before the opening of the play, when the divine Book of Nature stood security for the poet's all-too-human book of words, when the poet made raids on the already articulated, when perhaps God Himself could be conceived of as a silent but influential third member of any dialogue, as He was supposed to be in trials by combat. But *Richard II* also puts that time behind the poet and accepts with misgivings the fact that the order of men — uncertain, vulnerable, time-ridden — has substituted itself as the third member of dialogue and the guarantor of speech.[19] The

19 The appearance in 1961 of the third edition of Webster's New International Dictionary (Unabridged) marks the culmination of the war between "divine-right" and "statistical-might" conceptions of language. The editors, adopting the descriptive bias of modern structural linguists as against the prescriptive bias of traditional grammarians, radically reduce the number of qualitative distinctions and stylistic variants contained in earlier dictionaries and thus allow their authority as discriminators of verbal values to pass to the pop-

debasement of language, that "shabby equipment always deteriorating," that must follow on such a substitution cannot help but give
the poet pause.

ulace at large where it is expressed in the statistics of "usage." Deprived of
divine right, language is hard put to find even a substitute human authority,
and the danger is that whatever verbally is will become, under one vaguely
defined rubric of acceptance or another, right.

INDEX

Index

Abel, Lionel: and metatheatre, 4, 8–9

Abrams, Meyer: and metapoetics in Romantics, 15n

Acting: by characters in *Dream*, 130–132

Adams, Robert M.: and metadrama, 4n

Alexander, Peter: and *John*, 158n

Allegory: and metadramatic theme, 17–18

All's Well That Ends Well: "bed-trick" episode, 67

Aristotle: and poetics, 7; and plot as fate, 115n; and particularity of history, 158

Art: and nature, 10–11, 174; and time, 53–54; and reality, 80, 127–129, 145, 148; and language, 86, 174; and form, 91, 120–121, 127; and motion, 110; and dream, 138n, 140; as externalization, 141–143; as containment, 144–145; as communion, 147

Artaud, Antonin: and language of theater, 33n; and cruelty, 85

Auden, W. H.: and poetic speech, 52; and feudalism, 164n

Bacon, Francis: and language, 54–56; and empiricism, 170n

Barber, C. L., 69n, 125n, 126

Bible, 169

Boileau, Nicolas, 8

Bradbrook, M. C.: on *Titus*, 45

Brecht, Bertolt: and alienation effect, 12n, 45

Brooke, Arthur: and plot of *Romeo*, 113–116, 117n

Brower, Reuben: and metadramatic criticism, 5n

Brown, J. R.: and *Dream*, 136n

Büdel, Oscar: and aesthetic distance, 4n

Bulgarini, Bellisario: and relation of dream to art in Renaissance, 122–123

Bullough, Geoffrey, 118n

Burckhardt, Sigurd: and metadrama, 8n; and meaning in Shakespeare, 18n; and corporealization of words, 56n; and nominalism in *Romeo*, 88n; and symmetry of form in *Romeo*, 116

Burke, Kenneth: and plot in Aristotle, 115n; and relation of poet to dream, 138n; and metadrama in *Richard II*, 151n; and relation of kingship to property, 165n; and constitutive power of language, 167n

Campbell, Lily B.: and Renaissance world order, 178n

Cassirer, Ernst: and myth in *Dream*, 129; and language in *Richard II*, 166–167, 173, 180n

Character: paradoxically free and fated in drama (*Romeo*), 115n

Charlton, H. B.: and *Dream*, 122

Chaucer, Geoffrey: "House of Fame," 83–84

Coleridge, Samuel T.: and metapoetry in *Ancient Mariner*, 15

Comedy, 47, 67, 81, 132

Commedia dell'arte: and *Dream*, 132
Commercialism: imagery of in *Romeo*, 108–109; in *Richard II*, 165n, 169, 184
Contextualism: and language, 13; in *Romeo*, 119, 120
Cope, Jackson I.: and metadrama, 4n
Coriolanus, 6
Craig, Hardin: and Renaissance world order, 178n
Curtius, Ernst, 4n

Dean, Leonard: and stage-state metaphor in *Richard II*, 179n
Dent, R. W.: and imagination in *Dream*, 136n
Dramatic form: in *Titus*, 37–41, 85; in *LLL*, 64, 77–81, 87; in *Romeo*, 109–120, 138–139; in *Dream*, 121, 130, 144–145
Duplexity: defined, 12; exemplified in *Macbeth*, 12–14; exemplified in journey forms, 14–15; exemplified in *John*, 16–17; in *Richard II*, 151ff

Edwards, Philip: and comic form in *LLL*, 77n
Eliot, T. S.: and *Titus*, 23, 36, 41; *Murder in the Cathedral*, 46; and poet's acquiring dramatic style, 153; and language, 185
Empson, William: and double plot in drama, 103
Epstein, Leslie: and metadramatic criticism, 4n

Forker, Charles: and metadramatic criticism, 5n
Form and content: fusion in metapoetry, 9
Foster, Richard: and metadramatic criticism, 5n
Frank, Joseph: and spatial form in literature, 56n
Frye, Northrop: and critics, 3; and metaphor, 129

Garnier, Robert: and neo-Senecan closet drama, 50
Goddard, Harold: and *Dream*, 122
Goethe, Johann: and allegory, 17–18
Golding, Arthur: translation of *Meta-*

morphoses, 23, 27, 29, 31, 37, 39; translation of *De Beneficiis*, 75n
Griffin, Alice: and Shakespearean sources, 118n

Hamlet, 14, 156: and word-act, 32; and revenge form, 36; and expressive power, 140
Hathaway, Baxter: and Renaissance criticism, 122n
Haydn, Hiram: and Renaissance world order, 178n
Henry IV, part I, 3–4, 184–185
Henry V, 114, 148, 176
Henry VI, part III, 144
Henslowe, Philip: and dating of *Titus*, 24
Hierarchical order: as theme in *Dream*, 124–127, 146–148; in language and cosmos, 166–167, 175, 178n, 181
Hopkins, Gerard Manley: and nominalism in *Romeo*, 88n; and poetic purity, 92
Horace, 8
Husserl, Edmund, 88n

Illusion: and metadrama, 11; in *Dream*, 127–148
Intentional fallacy: license to practice, 6
Ionesco, Eugène: and art-nature in drama, 12n

Johnson, Samuel: and Shakespeare's punning, 57
Jonson, Ben: art and nature in Shakespeare, 10–11; and dating of *Titus*, 24
Joyce, James: and "accidental" art, 10; and poetic shut-in, 26; and dramatic mode, 143

Kaske, R. E.: and aube in *Romeo*, 113n
Kaufman, Walter: and supposed existentialism in Shakespeare, 180n
Keats, John: and lyric silence, 91–92
Kermode, Frank: and *Dream*, 122
King John: and duplexity in plot, 16–17; and historical truth, 157–158
King Lear, 156
Knight, G. Wilson: and Richard's Pomfret soliloquy, 175
Kraus, Karl: and verbal purity, 52, 55

Krieger, Murray: and metadramatic criticism of sonnets, 8n; and ekphrastic form in literature, 56n, 92, 110n; and personalism, 88n

Kyd, Thomas: and Senecan revenge drama, 37, 41; *Cornelia*, 50–51; and actionless drama, 50–51

La Guardia, Eric: and symbolism in *Richard II*, 178n

Language: and criticism, 18n; and barbarity, 29; and theater, 29, 33n, 76; and poet, 52, 74–75, 102, 150ff, 180–186; and time, 53ff, 80, 102, 139, 150; substantializing of, 54, 56–57, 60, 77, 84; and purity, 55, 88n, 94, 102–107; and sexuality, 57–60, 75–76; and community, 61–62, 66, 71, 73–74, 76; and money, 68, 108–109, 163–164; and decorum, 71; and action in drama, 72, 77–81; referential use of, 73n, 82, 86; as voiced expression, 81–84; and nominalism in *Romeo*, 87–91, 108; and silence, 91–97, 107–108; and sacraments in *Romeo*, 95–96; and verbal plagues in *Romeo*, 97–98; and dream in *Dream*, 138–141; and authority, 156, 175–176, 183; Cassirer's developmental phases of, 166–167, 173; and incarnation, 166–167; and constitutive power, 167n; and magical power, 167–169, 177, 184; and socio-political utility in *Richard II*, 171, 174, 181–184; devaluation of in *Richard II*, 184

Lévi-Strauss, Claude: and constitutive power of words, 167n

Liberality: Shakespeare's use of doctrine, 75n

Logos: in *Richard II*, 162–166, 170

Lovejoy, Arthur O.: and chain of being, 178n

Love's Labour's Lost, 157: analysis of, 52–84

Lyric: in *LLL*, 71–72, 73, 77, 78, 80; in *Romeo*, 91–97, 101–102, 106–107, 112–113, 150; in *Dream*, 142; in *Richard II*, 151–156

Macbeth: and Banquo's ghost, 12–14

Mack, Maynard: and metadramatic criticism, 4n; and tragic style, 104

MacLeish, Archibald: and metapoetry ("Ars Poetica"), 8, 9

Mahood, M. M.: and metadramatic criticism, 8n; and Elizabethan attitudes toward words, 167n

Masque: influence on *Dream*, 127–128

Matchett, William H.: and *John*, 158n

Maxwell, J. C.: and *Titus*, 24, 42

Mazzoni, Giacopo: and relation of dream to art in Renaissance, 122–123

Meaning: complexity of in Shakespeare, 17–18; and substance in words, 73n, 83–84; and name in *Richard II*, 172; and poet's task, 180–181

Measure for Measure: "bed-trick" episode, 67; and nature's liberality, 75

Meres, Francis: and *Titus*, 24

Metadrama: definition of, 4ff; summary of in plays treated, 20–21

Metamorphosis: in *Dream*, 129

Metaphor: and metadrama, 5, 15, 17; and allegory, 17–18; and *Dream*, 129–130, 138; and *Richard II*, 171, 174–180

Metapoetry, 8ff

Metatheatre: of Lionel Abel, 4ff

Midsummer Night's Dream, A, 11n, 13–14: analysis of, 120–148

Milton, John: and poetic silence ("Lycidas"), 91

Mimesis: and audience, 13–14; and Bulgarini, 123; and *Dream*, 137; and history, 157–158; and language in *Richard II*, 166, 173, 179

Myth: in *Dream*, 129, 137, 139

Nabokov, Vladimir: and author's relation to his work, 7

Nasser, Eugene Paul: and metadramatic criticism, 8n

Nicolson, Marjorie: and Renaissance world order, 178n

Nietzsche, Friedrich: and *Dream*, 128–129

Nominalism: in *Romeo*, 87–91

Olson, Paul A.: and hierarchy in *Dream*, 125n

Ong, Walter: and aural-visual in poetry, 56n, 81–84

Orpheus, 28–30, 150

Ovid: *Metamorphoses* (Golding's translation), 23, 27, 29, 31, 37, 39;

Orpheus, 28–30, 150; Philomela, 27, 34, 35, 39; style of, 34–35, 156

Palingenius, Marcellus, 123n
Pembroke, Countess of: and dramatic form, 50–51
Pepys, Samuel: opinion of *Dream*, 121
Petrarchan mode: in *LLL*, 68; in *Romeo*, 89–90, 95, 98–99, 155
Philomela, 27, 34, 35, 39
"Phoenix and the Turtle, The," 118
Platonism: and metapoetry, 9; and allegory, 17–18; and *Romeo*, 119; and *Dream*, 122; and *Richard II*, 173
Plautus, 156
Poetics: and metadrama, 7ff
Pope, Alexander, 8, 130
Price, H. T.: and *Titus*, 39–40, 48
Prior, Moody: and voyage motif in *Romeo*, 110

Rabkin, Norman: and metadramatic criticism, 5n, 11n, 136n
Rape of Lucrece, The: and narrative mode, 35
Ravenscraft, Edward: and *Titus*, 23–24
Richard II: analysis of, 149–186
Righter, Anne: and metadramatic criticism, 4n, 5; and *LLL*, 77n
Robbe-Grillet, Alain: and anthropomorphism in literature, 180n
Roethke, Theodore: "Light Listened," 17; "The Waking," 181
Romeo and Juliet, 157: analysis of, 85–119

Sargent, R. M.: and *Titus*, 42
Satire: in *LLL*, 72–73, 74
Seneca: revenge drama structure, 37–41; influence on *Titus*, 37, 48, 156; doctrine of liberality, 75n
Shakespeare, William, *see* specific titles
Shapiro, Karl: and metapoetry, 8
Sonnets (Shakespeare): no. *15*, 55; no. *23*, 145, 150; no. *55*, 150; no. *65*, 133; no. *66*, 41; no. *111*, 25
Spencer, Theodore: and Renaissance world order, 178n
Spenser, Edmund: and duplexity in *The Faerie Queene*, 14–15

Stirling, Brents: and haste in *Romeo*, 111n
Stroup, Thomas B.: and metadramatic criticism, 4n
Style: in *Titus*, 34–35; in *LLL*, 68; in *Romeo*, 89–91, 94–107, 150; in *Richard II*, 151–156
Swift, Jonathan: and journey form, 14; and language, 55

Taming of the Shrew, The, 131n, 145n
Tempest, The, 11n, 13n, 156
Thayer, C. G.: and metadramatic criticism, 5n
Theater: and metadrama, 11; and playwright, 26, 155, 181; and language, 33n, 76, 155; and audience, 136, 139, 142, 182; and *Richard II*, 168, 179n
Titus Andronicus, 156–157: and allegory, 17–18; analysis of, 23–51
Tragedy: in *Romeo*, 103–104, 108
Troilus and Cressida, 135

Venus and Adonis, 25–26, 50, 156
Vivas, Eliseo: and aesthetic experience in *Dream*, 147–148; and cultural values in *Richard II*, 169n
Vows: in *Titus*, 32, 38, 42–46; in *LLL*, 60–61, 64–66, 67, 70; as metadramatic indices in *Titus* and *LLL*, 85–86; in *Romeo*, 89–91
Vyvyan, John: and *Dream*, 122

Waith, Eugene M.: and Ovidian style in *Titus*, 34n
Warren, Robert Penn: and metapoetry in Coleridge, 15; and *Romeo*, 103; and *Dream*, 147
Webber, Joan: and symbolism in *Richard II*, 178n
Weidhorn, Manfred: and denomination in Shakespeare, 88n
Weisinger, Herbert: and metadramatic criticism, 4n
Wellek, René: and metapoetics, 8
Will: and grace as theme in *LLL*, 63n
Wind, Edgar: and Seneca's doctrine of liberality, 75n
Winter's Tale, The, 11n, 127, 156

Yates, F. A.: and *LLL*, 63n
Young, David: and imagination in *Dream*, 123n